THE LUMINOUS VISION

M
A
N
D
A
L
A

Anne Bancroft spent her childhood in the Quaker village of Jordans. When her four children were growing up, she began a personal quest for spiritual understanding. She is a vice-president of the World Congress of Faiths and was formerly lecturer in English and Comparative Religion at Hammersmith College for Further Education, London.

She is the author of *Religions of the East* (1974), *Twentieth Century Mystics and Sages* (1976), *Zen: Direct Pointing to Reality* (1980), *The Luminous Vision: Six Medieval Mystics* (1981), *The Buddhist World* (1984), *The New Religious World* (1985), *Festivals of the Buddha* (1985) and *Origins of the Sacred* (1987), and has recently finished a book of modern women mystics to be published in September 1989. She has made a number of broadcasts on mysticism on both television and radio.

THE LUMINOUS VISION

Six Medieval Mystics
and their Teachings

ANNE BANCROFT

M A N D A L A

UNWIN PAPERBACKS

London   Boston   Sydney   Wellington

First published in Great Britain by George Allen & Unwin Ltd, 1982

First published in paperback by Unwin® Paperbacks,
an imprint of Unwin Hyman Limited, in 1989

Unwin Hyman Limited
15–17 Broadwick Street
London W1V 1FP

Allen & Unwin Inc.
9 Winchester Terrace, Winchester, MA 01890, USA

Unwin Hyman Inc.
8 Winchester Place, Winchester, MA 01890, USA

Allen & Unwin New Zealand Pty Ltd in association with the
Port Nicholson Press
Compusales Building, 75 Ghuznee Street, Wellington, New Zealand

ISBN 0-04-440524-3

British Library Cataloguing in Publication Data

Bancroft, Anne
   The luminous vision.
   1. Christian life. Mysticism, history –
   Biographies – Collections
   I. Title
   248.2′2′0922

Printed and bound in Great Britain by
Cox & Wyman Ltd, Reading

Dedicated to my teachers, present and past

Contents

THE LUMINOUS VISION

Introduction

What is a mystic? In medieval Europe a mystic was someone who experienced inner or 'secret' knowledge of God. This knowledge was recognised at once as utterly different from anything previously known and yet at the same time more real and right than all other states. It was felt as taking place at a different level of being from the ordinary processes of thought and feeling and the mystic was aware of himself and others in a new way. It was as though a clarity – distinct altogether from the reasoning mind – had become revealed as the true basis of his person and of all the world. Such a state was alluded to by St Augustine when he said: "My mind in the flash of a trembling glance came to Absolute Being – That which Is."

The world as it is – not seen as we usually see it through the coloured spectacles of feeling and thought – but seen with the naked eye of clarity, revealed itself to the mystic as complete and perfect. "The spirit possesses God essentially in naked nature, and God the spirit" says Ruysbroeck. The more the mystic was able to live such clarity, the closer his words and actions corresponded to reality.

The word 'secret' then did not mean something obscurely mysterious nor did it mean anything supernatural or irrational. For mysticism has nothing to do with dark mystification, rather it is a way of illumination and light. 'Secret' in the medieval sense meant the insight which can only be experienced in a deeply inner way and which goes so far beyond the range of ordinary language that it can only be expressed by means of paradox and symbolism.

The medieval mystic seems to have known a direct contact and communication with something more real than is experienced in everyday human life, a reality which infinitely transcended his feeling of himself. This ineffable reality was the source to him of a wonderful certainty and joy. By means of its quickening power he became fully at home in the world, at

1

one with what was, and able to be at rest in self-giving love.

One great overriding question has always confronted man – the question of how to overcome separateness, how to find union, how to transcend one's own individual life and find 'at-one-ment' – in a word, how to be. For there often seems an unbridgeable gap between ordinary life and what Meister Eckhart called the "Nameless Nothing" and "God's 'isness', free from becoming". But that great gulf, that seemingly utter difference, becomes no difference at all in the mystic who really lives his true ground. So clearly is he illumined by his knowledge, that he is fully at peace with the world and able to be a very concrete and highly practical person, holding an easy balance and keeping all things in healthy perspective. Time and place, according to Eckhart our worst enemies because of our attachment to them, can be seen in their right relation to timelessness and infinity by means of a full awareness of the present moment. "God creates the world and all things in an ever-present Now" said Eckhart, and repeated it even more tellingly: "He who stands continually in a present Now, in him God the father begets his Son without ceasing."

Attention to this moment now prevents the mystic from being over-concerned with psychological or psychic states, or even with the fascinating vistas of philosophy. His goal is ultimate reality or nothing. When St Augustine exclaimed: "My life shall be a *real* life, being wholly full of Thee!" he was venting the belief that this conditioned world and the conditioned creature, when taken by themselves, are not fully real at all; not ultimate in any way. And that a life which merely consists of the interaction between these two leaves man's innate longing for absolute beingness unsatisfied.

"I would drink for a space of the unmingled wine" says Mechthild of Magdeburg. She expresses that hunger for unconditioned reality which is the driving force of the mystic; the longing which perhaps we all feel for existence as it is experienced when the mind is still and the heart surrendered, when the onlooker disappears and the seeming barrier between subject and object drops away.

Throughout recorded history there have always been people who move away from the social life of their times and spend their lives searching for an apparently mysterious and elusive sense of being; and who, this inner beingness found, live it, knowing the world in a new way, as if in a new dimension. Their relation to the world is altogether changed, for the realisation they have found is of a non-individual nature, transcending the hard separateness of me and mine which makes of man an isolated, time-bound and finite thing. Such longing for the completeness of real life shows that in so far as we are without that completeness we 'are' not. Although we can all potentially 'be', not many of us 'are'. For most of us life is a succession of occasions for putting on one set of clothes or another, all clearly intended to tell the beholder what we *think* we are. There are racial clothes and clothes called isms, as well as the more simple clothes of stockbroker, trade unionist or Member of Parliament – and parent, child and lover. Sometimes, however, it appears as though these sets of clothes march about the world with nobody inside them. The person 'is' not, he is merely his clothes.

It is hard. In order to 'be' we must be free, not determined either by nature or by society. As long as we are determined by 'outside' there can be no freedom. So we have to turn our backs on our conditioning, on our known world, in order to find a new way of being – to find what Krishnamurti, a mystic of this century, calls 'the innocent mind'. The innocent mind is able to live fully in the present without attachment to the past, for it is in the present moment that we are free – so long as we keep it clear of past and future – and it is then that we are most clearly our true selves.

A mystic, then, is one who is on the path to being truly what he is, in his most transcendent innerness. The more he is himself, the more he is 'real' and able to be at one with all creatures. He is no longer apart from the world and his awareness of reality is not something that has to be cultivated outside his ordinary everyday life. On the contrary, it is the very source of that meaning and purpose which makes outer life worth while.

The great revelation, common to the medieval mystics (and to mystics of all religions) but sadly undeveloped in Christianity since, was that all things have their being through the God-ground of existence. That which is, is God. So to find the reality of oneself is also to find God. Not so much the God of

3

symbol and image but what Julian of Norwich called 'the God that is unmade'. She says: "We need to have knowledge of the littleness of creatures and to naughten all thing that is made, for to love and have God that is unmade. For this is the cause why we are not all in ease and heart and soul: that we seek here rest in those things that be so little, wherein is no rest, and know not our God that is . . . the very Rest." Eckhart echoed this in his own uniquely straightforward language, saying: "God's characteristic is being . . . for in being, mere being, lies all that is. Being is the first name. Defect means lack of being. Our whole life ought to be being. So far as our life is feeble but taking it as being, it excels anything life can ever boast. I have no doubt of this, that if the soul had the remotest notion of what being means she would never waver from it for an instant. The most trivial thing perceived in God, a flower for example, would be a thing more perfect than the universe. The vilest thing present in God as being is better than angelic knowledge." And in a profound yet simple simile, Jan van Ruysbroeck says: "For, as the air is penetrated by the brightness and heat of the sun and iron is penetrated by fire; so that it works through fire the work of fire, since it burns and shines like fire; and so likewise can it be said of the air – for, if the air had understanding it could say: 'I enlighten and brighten the whole world' – yet each of these keeps its own nature. For the fire does not become iron, and the iron does not become fire, though their union is without means; for the iron is within the fire and the fire within the iron; and so also the air is in the sunshine and the sunshine in the air. So likewise is God in the being of the soul; and whenever the soul's highest powers are turned inwards with active love, they are united with God *without means*, in a simple knowledge of all truth, and in an essential feeling and tasting of all good."

In so far as such direct and immediate understanding can have an origin or tradition, it is widely accepted that the works of Dionysius the Areopagite – an unknown, probably Syrian, monk of the early sixth century, who gave himself the name of one of the followers of St Paul – had a great effect on the medieval mystics. This is undoubtedly true; but it may also be that all mystics, when they reach a certain level of understanding, concur; and that *The Mystical Theology*,

Dionysius' key work, was greeted with joy and fervour not only because it taught something unknown but also because it stated in sublime language that which was already well known.

Dionysius taught the negative way. That is to say, he believed that when we give names and attributes to 'the absolute No-thing which is above all existence' we lose its reality. Our mind can never know its Source while it scurries about taking the limited human intellect as the boundary of all knowledge – like one who searches for the sun inside the house instead of leaving the house behind and walking out into the clear, warm air. It is only through denying to ourselves all self-created images of God and all ideas about him, that we can become empty enough for the reality of God to make itself known to us. If we must use symbols, Dionysius says, then we should take our pointers from the ordinary world, for even such an inadequate representation of God as a lion, a bear, a leopard, or even a worm, is better than a more abstruse symbol because by its very inadequacy it leads man more quickly away from itself to transcendent Being, whereas those images which appeal more to the imagination may cause the mind to be content with the image and prevent it leaving it behind.

A warm, rich, satisfying symbol is all too easily clung to. Emotions are not regarded any more highly than conceptual ideas in such a mystic's journey to the God-ground. Man must let go of all knowledge and all experiences too, even visionary and heavenly ones, says Dionysius. He must go out into a 'dark unknowing' in ignorance. This is "the truly mystical darkness of unknowing in which he [Moses, as the prototype of the mystic] shuts out all intellectual apprehensions and remains entirely in the impalpable and invisible, belonging completely to him who is above all things, for he no longer belongs to anyone whether to himself or to another, but having renounced all knowledge, is united to the Unknowable in a better way, and knowing nothing, knows with a knowledge surpassing the intellect".

Dionysius' negative way – akin to the Hindu 'not this, not that' of Brahman – can also be called the way of freedom since we negate, or leave behind, all *bondage* to ideas and feelings. It does not lead to a vague nothingness but results in a state which Dionysius paradoxically likened to a statue – "For this is truly to see and to know, and superessentially to praise the Superessential; just as those who make a statue from the rough stone first remove all the superfluous matter that hinders the pure vision of the hidden form and thus reveal the hidden beauty *merely by this removal*." In other words, too readily do we believe that God is foreign to us, not realising that it is we who are foreign to ourselves, and that when we banish the accretions of self-image which have hidden our true nature from us the God-ground of ourselves will be revealed by the mere removal. Thus the end of the negative way is entirely positive, as it is in such other 'negative' religions as Buddhism and Hinduism.

The Mystical Theology was translated in the ninth century by John Scotus Erigena, often called John the Scot, whose own mystical understanding was profound. Its circulation strongly affected the thinking of the medieval mystics, particularly since they believed Dionysius actually to have been St Paul's disciple of the same name. Some passages in *The Cloud of Unknowing*, for instance, appear to be very close in feeling to *The Mystical Theology* – "Lift up your heart unto God with a meek stirring of love and mean himself and none of his goods. And thereto look that you loathe to think on anything but himself so that naught work in your mind nor in your will but only himself. And do that in you to forget all the creatures that ever God made and the works of them, so that your thought or your desire is not directed or stretched to any of them, neither in general nor in special." The three essential beliefs of mysticism – that the beingness of oneself is also that of the God-ground, or timeless Reality; that to find this unconditioned beingness we have to let go our dependence on conditioned things; and that actually to do this reveals to us the nature of our true life as a human being – these three beliefs are not only those of Dionysius and the Christian mystics who followed him but also the basic beliefs of all religions, particularly Buddhism – indeed the Four Noble Truths are echoed time and again in medieval words.

The medieval mystics, then, who trod this universal path knew with certainty how to distinguish reality from fantasy. Nowadays the word 'mysticism' is often used for occult or magical powers. But such a misuse is not helpful, for the spheres are totally different. Contemplative mysticism is about the ineffable and inexhaustible mystery of existence itself, whereas magic is the discovery and manipulation of the elemental forces of the world. As Berdyaev says: "Mysticism is union with God, magic with the spirits of nature. . . . Mysticism is the sphere of liberty, magic of necessity. Mysticism is detached and contemplative, magic is active and militant; it reveals the secret forces of humanity and of the world without being able to reach the depths of their divine origin. Mystical experience constitutes precisely a spiritual deliverance from the magic of the natural world, for we are fettered to this magic without always recognising it."

The 'don't-know-mind' (also an essential part of Eastern religion) is the first necessity of contemplative mysticism. When everything is thought to be known then the world appears a dead and even hostile place. But when such 'knowledge about' is shown to be of its very nature limited and superficial, a great unknowing takes place and every object is seen afresh as intrinsically mysterious and awesome. The nature of the universe and the nature of oneself are experienced as one in this unknowing and a feeling of shattering amazement arises that the real self is not what it was always thought to be, but something utterly different in nature. "The seer and the seen," says Plotinus, another influential precursor of the medieval mystics, "the subject and the object – it is a daring assertion – are one. Then the seer neither sees nor distinguishes them as two nor imagines them apart. He is utterly changed, no longer himself, no longer self-belonging. He belongs to God and is one with him like two circles which have one centre: they are one when they coincide, two only when they separate."

The true mystic, then, is one who is freed from the feelings of oppression and insecurity which arise when we regard the world as alien to us and ourselves as being directed by it from without. In mysticism everything is experienced and lived out from a deep sense of the inner self, knowing it to be the miraculous God-ground, and the expression of this living is in spontaneous and joyful self-giving. Real loving is easy when it is seen that there is nothing external to oneself, nothing alien or strange or impenetrable, but rather a world which is utterly and intimately oneself. "How can one describe it as other than oneself," asks Plotinus, "that which when one saw it seemed one with oneself?"

Such insight hardly needs the formal doctrines of religion to help it and indeed the mystics, particularly Eckhart, made no bones about proclaiming the Ground as beyond all theology: "You shall know him [God] without image, without semblance and without means – 'But for me to know God thus, with nothing between, I must be all but he, he all but me' – I say, God must be very I, I very God, so consummately one that this he and this I are one 'is', in this is-ness working one work eternally; but so long as this he and this I, to wit, God and the soul, are not one single here, one single now, then I cannot work with nor be one with that he."

To know God 'without means' – for that sort of statement Eckhart was brought to trial for heresy. The attitude of the medieval Church towards its mystics was one of suspicion and bare tolerance – indeed towards such outspoken groups as the Friends of God there was no toleration at all and many of their writings were destroyed, or rewritten with the intention of making them appear heretical and scandalous.

Indeed the background to the lives of the mystics was one of fearful tensions. When John the Scot brought the mystical teachings of Dionysius to light in the ninth century, the Church was taken unawares and did not know how to fight a concept of God which seemed alien to Western theology. It was puzzled rather than condemnatory. Nobody could understand John and in the three centuries following he was buried in oblivion, although a legend was kept dimly alive that he had founded the two universities of Oxford and Paris and that he was killed at the Malmesbury School by being stabbed to death by the pens of his pupils.

But by the end of the twelfth century, the situation was changing for the worse. A theologian of the University of Paris called Amaury discovered *Periphyseon*, a book written by John Scotus, and taught it to his pupils. A spiritual bombshell burst in France. Amaury taught "that every man ought to believe, as an article of his faith, without which there is no salvation, that each one of us is a member of the Christ". Such an 'article of faith' drew forth the instant hostility of the Church. He was quickly condemned by the university authorities for teaching a dangerous new theology, and his subsequent appeal to the Pope was turned down. It is said he died of heartbreak shortly afterwards. But, as with all good teachers, the quickening power of his thoughts could not be suppressed and a few years later a group of intelligent men and women, both lay and religious, formed itself in Paris to propagate his ideas. They announced that God is not far away but has his real being in the lives of all those who can become open to his presence. As soon as a person was aware of God's life within him, then he was no longer bound by the rules and rites which are only necessary for those on a lower spiritual level. The greatest joy to be known, they maintained, was to find oneself at one with God, and in order to arrive at this experience the members of the society practised silent meditation and heightened awareness of the inner Presence.

At last the Church was fully roused. The society was infiltrated, spied on and denounced. Convicted of heresy, its members were stripped of their clerical robes before the gawping crowds and many were burnt at the stake. In 1209 a Council ordered Amaury's bones to be disinterred and burnt. Books by Aristotle and others were condemned and joined the general bonfire, but all to no avail. The ideas brought forward by Amaury continued to circulate and his secret disciples believed that they were the founders of a new spiritual age, one which rejected the traditional role of the Church and all its rites and ceremonies and its worship of saints. Compassion and understanding were more important than any sacrament, they taught.

"They denied", says Chronicler Caesar of Heisterbach, "the resurrection of the body. They taught that there is neither heaven nor hell, as places, *but that he who knows God possesses heaven*, and he who commits a mortal sin carries hell within himself just as a man carries a decayed tooth in his mouth. They treated as idolatry the custom of setting up statues to saints, and of burning incense to images. They laughed at those who kissed the bones of martyrs."

Those who could be caught were burned at the stake and this caused a wide dispersement of the movement into Germany, southern France and Italy. Links were formed with other

9

groups and new sects rose and fell. Some, with an emphasis on ecstatic trances and what sound remarkably like tantric practices, appear to have been borderline hysterics, but the courage to live a life of spiritual freedom can only be admired.

It is in this explosive thirteenth century that the move to individuality and the revolt from authoritarianism seemed to make itself fully felt. Many, whether within or without the Church, came to express a growing feeling that mankind had lost the way and that the simple teaching of Christ had been buried beneath the structure of the Church.

A 'back to Christ' feeling began to grow and found expression in one of the most idealistic movements Christianity has yet seen – the Sisterhood of the Beguines and the Brotherhood of the Beghards. The movement had started quietly with the creation of the Beguines in the twelfth century, an act which was both economic and compassionate. The terrible Crusades and the wars of central Europe had taken such a toll of male lives that every town and village had its hordes of wretched women, who, left without protectors and with no means of livelihood except prostitution, begged their food daily from the market place – "Bread for God's sake" (*Brod durch Gott*). In 1180 a certain stammering (hence his name) priest of Flanders called Lambert le Begue, out of pity for these ragged and starving victims of battle, gathered a number together, both virgins and widows, and settled them in a large house. They were to live a religious life but as lay people, thus having the sheltered advantages of the convent but without its restrictions. Soon the Sisterhood of the Beguines, as they were called after le Begue, began to grow. Settlements of houses were built and came to be known as Beguinages.

The growing number of women who found a refuge there also found a new life. There was leisure for meditation and prayer; there was the feeling of sharing in a family atmosphere; there was social life; and there were jobs and responsibilities to keep them occupied. So popular did the movement become that by the middle of the thirteenth century every city had societies of Beguines. And with the impetus of the 'back to Christ' movement men too were following their example and forming associations called Beghards (from which comes our word 'beggar'). The Beghards became groups of religious laymen who went about the country doing good in whatever way they could. They took care of the sick and the mad, preached in the local tongue, and buried the dead. They lived partly from begging and partly from working.

It was too good to last. As early as 1244 the Church was showing alarm at the freedom and independence given to the Beguines and by the end of the century they were being regarded by the ecclesiastical authorities as a thorough pest. They were very popular with the people, much more so than the orders of friars, and consequently their begging reaped a bigger harvest. Their burials and masses were conducted without clergy and so there were no fees to be gained for the Church. They had no vows of obedience to keep and yet they lived as though following the religious life, wearing special robes and acknowledging superiors only among themselves. They preached on profound and sacred subjects, such as the Holy Trinity, but what they said was thought to be undermining faith in the Church and indeed to be endangering the salvation of many.

With this mixture of jealousy and possessive righteousness it was inevitable that the Church should do its best to smother the Beguines and the Beghards. They were called heretical and in 1306 the Archbishop of Cologne issued an edict against them. However, threats of excommunication availed nothing. In fact the edict brought about the opposite of its aim. The Beguines and Beghards, seen to be victimised for what was regarded by many as a simple true Christianity, grew in such numbers that the Franciscans and Dominicans were severely decreased.

They were well suited to spread the ideas of Amaury and these ideas began to be known as the doctrine (or heresy, depending on your viewpoint) of the Free Spirit. The societies of Beguines and Beghards, among which were a number of highly intelligent and thoughtful people, came to be called the Brethren of the Free Spirit and suddenly the Church found itself facing a greater threat than it could ever have foreseen.

The central ideas of the Brethren were clear. God is everything. From oneness he goes forth into differentiation and plurality. In this state of multiplicity he is to be found in all that is real. The end of all things is to be 'oned' with him once more in divine unity, and man's path is to become free of himself so that God will do all in him that is necessary. There is therefore no need for the Church because man himself is the revelation of God. God is as much man as he is the consecrated bread and wine.

Such a challenge to the supremacy of the Church could only be met by the most extreme measures and these were taken. The persecution of the Beguines and the Beghards was decreed in 1311, although there was a long delay in putting it into practice because there were many loyal and virtuous Catholics among them and it seemed impossibly difficult to single out those to whom the decree should apply.

In fact it had little effect on the Beghards, who could look after themselves and move freely to other countries. But the Beguines were devastated. Deprived of their Beguinages and turned out into the world with no support and with those who would have helped them also at risk of persecution, many died of starvation. And then, with the growing power of the Inquisition, the Beghards too were decimated. There was no hope for any brotherhood or sisterhood outside the Church and many were caught and burned at the stake.

Such was the background to the mysticism of the thirteenth and early fourteenth centuries, a spiritual and psychological landscape which deeply affected such mystics as Jan van Ruysbroeck (whose letter to a group of Beguines is one of the most beautiful and profound writings known in mysticism), and Meister Eckhart. But that period, turbulent enough, was to pale in comparison with the woes and disasters of the later fourteenth century. Our own times seem chaotic to us but the Middle Ages were much worse.

The Church, to which the ordinary man turned for guidance, was so split by warring factions that its very existence might be considered as one of the more harmful influences of the time. From 1309 to 1377 was the era of the 'Babylonish Captivity' of the Church, when the papal seat was established at Avignon and the popes became puppets of France. For many this was a traumatic calamity but it was followed by a still worse misfortune. When Pope Gregory XI died in 1378 so great was the strife within the Church that there was a double election, resulting in two rival popes, and for the next forty years the

Church was torn in two by the 'Great Schism' which lasted until 1417.

Preceding this disastrous event was a similar political situation in Germany when in 1314 a double election of Emperors took place. Louis of Bavaria was chosen by one party and Frederick of Austria by another. The Pope took Frederick's side, excommunicated Louis, and laid an interdict on all the cities which had supported him. By this interdict all public religious services were prohibited. This meant that in many parts of Germany the mass was not celebrated, babies were unbaptised, and the dying were refused the consolation of the last rites.

As though the snarlings of corrupt men were not enough, nature joined in with violent earthquakes throughout the Rhine valley. In the middle of the fourteenth century the city of Basle came crashing down in a heap of ruins and many other cities were also affected.

But the greatest and most terrible cause of havoc in that torn and bewildered century was nature's cruellest blow – the Black Death. People saw it as God's wrath. It first struck Europe in 1347, where it raged for two years, then came back in slightly milder form in 1358 and 1363. The Black Death, which brought with it the horrific stench of decay, houses marked with a cross and bloated corpses, killed a large part of the population, in some areas reducing it to a tenth.

Thus for two centuries western Europe was a battlefield, red with the blood of the victims of wars, rebellions, persecutions and plagues. Not only were emperors at war but so too were the small princes, dukes and nobles of the country; and frequently their reigns were so cruel that insurrections broke out among the people. In many areas the countryside was laid waste and those who did not die by the sword perished of starvation or plague. The Church, intent only on its internal power struggles, provided little in the way of help or consolation, and slid further and further into a morass of immorality and corruption, achieving eventually its foulest example in Pope Alexander VI (1492), the notorious Roderigo Borgia, among whose crimes were perjury, poisoning and robbery.

Yet, contrasting with this deeply dyed background was the

clarity of the mystics, who, while never shunning the strife and tragedy around them, yet concentrated on the inner life and thus brought perspective and balance into the hearts of all who knew them.

How this situation compares with our own era is plain to see. Our century too is notorious for persecution, cruelty and murder, from the horror-filled concentration camps of Germany to the devastation of Nagasaki and the petrol-soaked forests of Vietnam. Our existence is still rent asunder by the abyss we ourselves create between what we do and what we are. We have not yet come to a state of self-knowledge which grounds us in reality and from which our actions can arise directly from our whole self. We live fragmented in our nature, not complete, unable to find a whole and total perspective. When we focus this split and divided perspective on our problems we get a fragmented solution to which we devote all our attention and energy. It is just this incompleteness, this lack of wholeness, which leads to unhappiness. But because we are ignorant of our own fragmentation we project all our dissatisfactions on to the world and blame the world for all our troubles. Then follows the build-up of arms (on which the world spends far more than on health) and yet more persecutions and wars and bitter hatred between man and man.

In this century, too, Christianity may fairly be said to be rent still by schisms. There is no longer persecution or vicious corruption – for this we may truly be thankful – but instead there is a strange malaise. One could call it a grinding to a halt, the juddering of an engine running out of fuel. The emphasis is not on God any longer but – supposedly – on man. And yet it is not man in his wholeness that present-day Christianity seems to be concerned with, but man's physical and social needs. Yet 'man cannot live by bread alone' and there is as great a hunger for truly spiritual leadership today as there was in the thirteenth and fourteenth centuries.

The England of the fourteenth century, like Britain today, was somewhat apart from its continental neighbours and did not suffer quite such agonies and storms as swept through central Europe. Yet England thought of itself essentially as part of Europe and it shared in all the great movements originating there. There was a constant movement of the population between the countries and it is quite wrong to regard England in medieval times as slow-moving or static. Scholars and teachers, as well as those who were buying and selling, crossed and re-crossed the Channel in a steady stream, not conscious of nationalism as we know it today because there was one Church to which all belonged, however repressive and cruel that Church might be.

The background to the English mystics therefore has many things in common with that of the European ones. Yet it has a different feel: a stronger emphasis perhaps on personal independence and freedom, a love of simplicity and directness, a burning indignation at the ecclesiastical vices of the day. Somehow the English Church was already eating its way out of the Roman cocoon, as was the English language. Until the fourteenth century Latin was the universal tongue. But then, by parliamentary decree, English became the recognised language of the realm, inviting the uprush of a spring of poetry and debate. In this land of new beginnings the English mystics lived and worked and contemplated. Their prose had a strength and vitality which we rarely hear today. In spite of the Black Death, in spite of the brutish cruelty still to be found at all levels and the dirt and poverty, medieval England was Merrie England and kept a lighter touch than her continental cousins. This spirit is captured by Trevelyan:

"The closer we look at medieval England, the more we shall feel inclined to picture it as young, hardy and joyous. To begin with, the country was full of colour. The churches glowed with stained glass and painted walls; the dresses of the wealthy, men as well as women, were gorgeous and brilliant, and if the peasantry wore more serviceable russets and browns and blues, they usually managed to introduce a splash of red or other bright colour in their hoods or kerchiefs. And the country was full of song, and with this went dancing."

And so to the mystics themselves. The criterion for choice of these six was that each mystic should show that particular clarity of vision which bridges the gap between the everyday and the ineffable, helping us to transcend our own dualities and bringing us to our own experience of numinous existence. So the real theme of this book is one of transformation – of seeing ourselves in the light of these teachings.

This is not to say that each of these mystics is a perfect teacher – indeed it would be true to say that none of them is. But each has an individual way which will coincide with and perhaps amplify some aspects of our own knowledge and understanding.

For instance, Dame Julian and Rolle can claim kinship with a *religious* background. They lived and taught within their Christian beliefs and – certainly in the case of Julian – the teaching is a well-constructed and deeply mystical commentary on the basic doctrines of the medieval Church. Indeed so strong was *her* insight that she saw with ease how God is not only Father but Mother also – a point which will appeal to many of us today – and she was not afraid to speak of 'Jesus our Mother'. With great simplicity she states: "Our Saviour is true Mother, in whom we are endlessly born; and we shall never come out of him." And with a thoroughly medieval and yet psychologically sane and balanced view of the Trinity, she says:

"Our high Father, all-mighty God, who is Being, he knew us and loved us from before-any-time. Of which knowing, by his full marvellous deep compassion . . . he willed that the second Person should become our Mother, our Brother, and our Saviour. Wherefrom it follows that as truly as God is our Father, so truly God is our Mother. Our Father wills, our Mother works, our good Lord, the Holy Ghost confirms."

It can be seen, then, that she at least was happily at ease in her medieval life of contemplation. The symbol of her deepest mind was both male and female and all her writing is infused with this balance and maturity. In Taoist terms, both Yin and Yang were fully realised within her, bringing her to wholeness.

This cannot be said of all the mystics. Both Rolle and Ruysbroeck suffered in their own contemplative lives from enmities and petty jealousies, and even the serene author of the *Cloud* speaks impatiently at times of "young, presumptuous disciples who would, with curiosity born of imagination, pierce the planets and make a hole in the firmament to look in"; and he speaks as well of the pious people who live in their emotions and "travail their fleshly hearts outrageously in their breasts, and hurt full sorely the silly soul and make it fester in a feigned fantasy of fiends".

But all three managed, as did that soaring eagle-saint,

Bernard, during the course of their lives (and here we can only go by the evidence in his own works of the author of the *Cloud*) to overcome such natural but unconstructive irritations and negative feelings, and to see them – as a Tibetan Buddhist would see them – as excellent personal teachings. For your worst enemy is your best teacher, say the Buddhists, in that he is the one who really teaches you about your own reactions and thus helps you to overcome them. It was undoubtedly the positive cultivation of compassionate love – another link between Mahayanan and Christian teaching – which was the instrument by which the personality problems of the mystics were sublimated and transmuted. They came to a profound acceptance of life as it really is and in that acceptance a love for all existence could flower.

Even Rolle, the most cantankerous, ended his life in tranquillity and dignity, although we cannot in all honesty attribute to him Mother Julian's balance and calmness. He was, even more than she, enclosed by the medieval Christian tradition, although he was such an individualist that his life was lived altogether outside the Church. Indeed there has been controversy as to whether he was genuinely a mystic or not and it has been stated by some, such as Professor David Knowles, that he was really just a 'beginner'. But to agree would be to narrow down our views on mysticism merely to one single standard, that of Dionysius' 'unknowing'. Some of us may still see, when reading him, Rolle's experience of 'heat, melody and sweetness' and his devotional life of lyrical praise and love, as just the beginning of the path compared to the more serious states of self-free contemplation. But should we give ourselves such rigid boundaries as this? Should we become exact in the level of attainment we grant each mystic? Too much finicking nicety in the judgements we make will prevent us from appreciating their experiences in any real way. For there is surely space and time for delight and loving attention and joyful praise of that which is, as well as for the moments of 'unknowing'?

To reject Rolle might be to reject a vital part of ourselves. Admittedly he himself was a mixed personality, but his message is important for us because all too easily do we *refrain* from praise and adoration, believing that the mysticism of

17

darkness – the negative way of Dionysius – does not include the mysticism of light – an outward ecstasy. Yet these two ways are not opposed but belong together and we deny either to our cost. For the Sufis dance into trance states of union with the divine, the Hindus chant to the same effect, and the Greek Orthodox Church uses the prayer of Jesus (which Rolle also used) as a mantra for much the same purpose. Do we frown in superiority on all these superb ways? In the end we must surely agree, as Rolle himself pointed out, that there is a right way for everybody and that it is up to us to find it, but in so doing we should never reject the paths of others – which may indeed contribute greatly to our own.

In many ways the English mystics in particular did combine the light and dark mysticism, for they taught a religion of joyful simplicity. They were not obsessed with violence, morbidity, or hellfire, and they loved Christ more than they feared the Devil. They established, especially in the case of Julian and Rolle, a mysticism based on wonder, praise and worship; and revealed what Thomas Merton, a mystic of our own century, terms a 'paradise spirituality' – one which affirmed the innocence and 'merriness' of Christ.

But it is fair to accept a difference between the trio of Julian, Rolle and Bernard and the other three. The former trio – and the mighty Bernard basically belongs to this group although he shares some insights of the others – exhibits the 'illumined way', which is the term St John of the Cross uses to describe advanced mystical states. But he reserves the term 'unitive way' for those who have experienced a transforming union – and we do not find much evidence of this in, say, Rolle.

The unitive way is that of Ruysbroeck, Eckhart and the author of the *Cloud*. About them there is little to say for their own words speak for them. Whereas Julian, Rolle and Bernard give us mystical insights from a medieval background, these others have transcended their background and even their religion – Ruysbroeck speaks tellingly of the 'wayless way' and Eckhart was brought to trial for soaring above Christology. So their mysticism is largely released from form, and their teaching is practical yet sublime, individual yet timeless.

This book, then, shows two aspects of the mystical path, although they are not opposing aspects. As St Bernard – deeply aware of both – points out, they complement each other; and, with caution, we might say that one naturally develops into the other – the first into the second. For, as St Bernard also pointed out, real transcendence belongs in the end to the state where self is forgotten.

Finally it must be said that where modern English has served the interpretation better than either Middle or translated English, this has been used, although original texts have been adhered to as closely as possible.

Jan van Ruysbroeck

Each of the mystics in this book seems to have at least one outstanding quality which marks him off from all the others. In Jan van Ruysbroeck's case, it is harmony. His inward-looking nature was formed early in life, when he was still a young boy. He was born and spent his childhood in the village of Ruysbroeck from which he took his name, as was the custom at that time. This village (which is now a thriving town near Brussels) was then surrounded by forest and marshland. The forest came right up to the huts of the small hamlet and almost surrounded it except on the west, where the great marshes beyond the willow-bordered river glinted and shone like molten metal in the magnificent Flanders sunsets. To the young Jan both forest and sun held great mystery and meaning. The sun came to dominate his imagery so that in later life he often compared the clarity of the God-ground to the illumination of the sun: "It is as when you stand in the dazzling radiance of the sun, and turning away your eyes from all colour, from distinguishing all the various 'things' which the sun illumines, you simply follow with your eyes the brightness of the rays, and so are led up into the sun's very essence."

But it was the forests which drew him back and where he finally made his home. The great beech trees which soared upwards to the light, the greenness and silence, the evocative play of shadow and sunshine, the sighing of the wind through the branches – all these held an enchantment and numinous mystery for him and his later work shows the sense of wonder he felt. As well he loved all natural things in an ordinary way so that his written works are full of references to the countryside – the lessons drawn from the habits of ants and bees, the comparison of the surrendered soul to the sunflower ('one of nature's most wonderful works'); the Christians who are like three sorts of birds, those who prefer to hop about on the earth, those who swim far out on the waters, and those who soar up to the heavens. The wild exultant birds he saw on the marshes must have touched his imagination more than any other creature, for 'many-feathered' is the best name he can find for the contemplative on his journey to God.

Jan was an only child and had no father. It is thought that his father died when he was young but nothing is known of him. Jan's mother is said to have been a good woman, devoted to bringing up her son but finding the task a hard one and consequently over-anxious and possessive about him. She is described by the Augustinian canon, Pomerius, Jan's biographer, as over-solicitous and too loving, as well as being of somewhat limited intelligence. Country life at that time – he was born in 1293 – was boisterous and turbulent and Pomerius records that Jan had little liking for the rough games of the other children, the beery carousing of the adults, and the noisy strife and intimacy of a small village. He was too young for this to be an attitude of priggish affectation and was entirely sincere in his sensitive distaste for the drunkenness and gluttony he saw about him.

At the age of eleven he ran away. It was never discovered why he did this but from common human experience we can make a good guess. Many of us live very intensely as children. We are overwhelmingly aware of the mystery of existence. Our awe and wonder at the marvel of things creates a deepfelt inner life – one which at all costs must be kept secret from the derision of other children or the prying possessiveness of parents.

Perhaps Jan felt he could no longer bear life within such boundaries. Whatever his reasons we can be sure they were profound because all the rest of his life was peaceful, harmonious and orderly. And he did not run very far, only to Brussels, some few miles away. Here he went straight to his uncle, Jan Hinckaert, priest of the church of Saint-Gudule in Brussels.

He was welcomed joyfully. A strong bond of affection soon developed between the kindly priest and the mystical young boy. Perhaps Jan spoke of his inner world and of his need to follow the directions of his spirit. At all events, Hinckaert adopted him forthwith and undertook to educate him.

The first four years of Jan's education were spent at the

Latin school of Brussels where, from the records of that century, we know he must have studied grammar, dialectic, rhetoric, music, arithmetic, geometry and astronomy. Astronomy in particular he seems to have loved, for the movements of the planets form an important part of his teaching. There was a common belief in the fourteenth century, inherited from Greek thought, that the planets did in fact shape one's character – indeed belief in their pre-natal powers was absolute. Jan became passionately interested too in all the other natural forms of the universe. He investigated everything – mineralogy, botany, zoology, the motions of the tides, the way trees are grafted, the habits of ants and bees. It was through the forms and ways of the natural world that he hoped to lay hold of analogies which could be applied to the spiritual life, but it was the signs of the Zodiac which held his attention most strongly.

He saw the splendour and power of the sun (which he likened to the coming of Christ) when it rises in Gemini – "that is, the Twins; or a twofold thing of one nature" – as having a double power to quicken all that grows out of the earth, just as when the sun of Christ rises in the heart there is a double growth of natural goodness. When in Cancer – "which means Crab because it can go no further, but begins to go back" – the sun draws up all the moisture and the earth becomes dry and fruits ripen quickly, "so, likewise, when Christ the Divine Sun has risen to the zenith of our hearts – that is, above all the gifts and consolations and sweetness which we may receive from him . . . he will draw all things, that is, all our powers, to himself . . . to an inward constraining and drawing of the heart towards the most high unity of God."

But when "the visible sun enters the sign of Leo, that is, the Lion, who is fierce by nature for he is lord over all beasts; so, likewise, when a man comes to *this* way, Christ the bright Sun stands in the sign of the Lion, for the rays of his heart are so fierce that the blood in the heart of the impatient man must boil. And when this fierce way prevails, it masters and subdues all other ways and works; for it wills to be wayless, that is, without manner. . . . At times God grants to such men a sudden spiritual glimpse of strange brightness, shining forth from the simple Nudity. And thereby for an instant the spirit is raised above itself; but the light passes at once and the man returns to himself again. This is the work of God himself; it is something very sublime; for those to whom it happens often become illuminated men."

'The heart of the impatient man' – for some of us there seems to come a time when a great effort must be made, when nothing else will suffice but to find a new level of existence, one which can only be sensed by intuition, not foretold by the mind. Then there is a fierce impatience, a feeling that everything in life is trivial compared to the longing for the reality of the spirit. No ordered method of practice seems appropriate at that time. The leap must be wayless. And when it is so then the brightness lights up the nature of all things. "Though from my gaze profound, deep awe hath hid Thy face; in wondrous and ecstatic grace I feel Thee touch my inmost ground" said the medieval Sufi mystic, Al-Junaid.

The young Jan could not have had such insight during his school years and it was much later on in his life that he wrote about the Zodiac in his work *The Adornment of the Spiritual Marriage*. But his schooling gave him the knowledge which he later used to such good effect in his teaching analogies.

While he was still at school, his mother came to join him. News of his studiousness had reached her and made life without him intolerable. So she arrived in Brussels, having sold her few belongings, only to discover that she could not live with Jan since no woman was allowed to share a priest's house. Hinckaert found her a place in a beguinage and there she remained. Her nature sweetened in these new surroundings and she saw Jan frequently. The true bond between mother and son was re-established, perhaps helped by the growing respect the mother felt for her son's learning and understanding.

After his schooling was finished, there is a gap of some years in Jan's life of which we know nothing. Possibly he joined one of the bands of wandering students who went off each autumn to a university. More likely, though, he spent some time in Cologne with Tauler and Suso, disciples of Meister Eckhart, for his own thinking was greatly influenced by that powerful and penetrating master.

We next hear of him at the age of twenty-four, in 1317, when, rather later than usual, he was ordained as a priest, becoming a chaplain to his uncle. It was about then that his uncle, who was a good man but rich and worldly, had a transforming experience which was to affect both their lives.

Apparently he heard an inner voice directing him to hurry to his own church, Saint-Gudule. There he found a missionary priest, who had a speech defect and was known for his hesitancy, about to give a sermon. As soon as he saw Hinckaert he burst forth into such a flood of eloquence as he had never known before. He ended by remarking: "I believe that this ease with which I speak has been given to me because there is one in your midst who should mend his ways and turn to a better way of life." Hinckaert took this utterance as meant for himself and changed his way of life accordingly. The household became modest and simple. Hinckaert's conversion soon turned others in the same direction so that a small group formed itself around him. One who was most powerfully affected was another priest, Franco van Coudenberg, and a common desire for a way of life which would include simple renunciation as well as love and faith made the two priests decide to join forces and to give all their possessions to the poor, keeping for themselves only the bare necessities of life. In this way they and Jan lived and worked together and this association lasted for the rest of their lives.

For the next twenty-six years, that is until he was fifty, Jan worked as a busy priest in Brussels. He was cathedral chaplain in a thriving capital city and his time for contemplation must have been limited. Yet there is no doubting that he passed through some high mystical states during this time, although to the outer world he gave the impression, it is said, of a shabbily-dressed, dreamy priest 'going about the streets of Brussels with his heart lifted up unto God'.

What were his thoughts during these years? Undoubtedly the most essential understanding was soon born and took shape. There are two parts to this belief of Ruysbroeck's and they spring immediately from his strong intuition that the ultimate Reality is both Being and Becoming: onefold and changeless in essence, active and diverse in expression, impersonal and personal, undifferentiated and differentiated, transcendent and immanent, 'working without ceasing, for He is Pure Act'. So the first part of Ruysbroeck's twofold understanding is concerned with *finding* the infinite God-ground, and the second with *experiencing* it as man in the diversity of the world.

In the first part, Ruysbroeck introduces us to four stages of spiritual growth, all of which receive 'the gift of God'. The initial stage is the hireling of God – one feels that in Ruysbroeck's eyes it was rather a low state.

"Some men receive the gifts of God as hirelings, but others as faithful servants of God; and these differ from one another in all inward works, that is, in love and intention, in feeling, and in every exercise of the inward life.

"Now understand this well: all those who love themselves so inordinately that they will not serve God save for their own profit and because of their own reward, these separate themselves from God and dwell in bondage and their own selfhood; for they seek and aim at their own in all that they do. And therefore with all their prayers and all their good works, they seek after temporal things, or perhaps strive after eternal things for their own benefit and profit. These men are bent upon themselves in an inordinate way; and that is why they ever abide alone with themselves, for they lack the true love which would unite them with God and with all His beloved. And although these men seem to keep within the commandments of God and the Holy Church, they do not keep within the law of love; for all that they do, they do not out of love but out of sheer necessity lest they should be damned. And because they are inwardly unfaithful they dare not trust in God; but their whole inward life is doubt and fear, travail and misery . . . for they love themselves better than God and they love blessedness wholly for their own sakes. And therefore they dare not trust in God.

"But from that very hour in which, with God's help, such a man can overcome his selfhood – that is to say, when he is so detached from himself that he is able to leave in the keeping of God everything of which he has need – behold, through doing this he is so well pleasing to God that God bestows upon him His grace. And through grace he feels true love: and love casts out doubt and fear and fills the man with hope and trust, and thus he becomes a faithful servant and means and loves God in all that he does. Behold, this is the difference between the faithful servant and the hireling."

It is quite likely that in the fourteenth century people were not so attached to material things as they are today. Therefore it is only in one or two sentences that Ruysbroeck gives us a glimpse of that condition necessary for knowing what it is to truly love – detachment from our surroundings. To let go of our dependence on the outer world is often seen by non-mystical people as a difficult, scaring and even selfish thing to do. But it is the basis of all spiritual training. It has been universally found that to love people and things uncon-ditionally and only for themselves, which is true love, means that our involvement with them has to come to an end. Ruysbroeck looks upon the ceasing of such involvement as an act of will on our part – 'when man is so detached from himself that he is able to leave in the keeping of God everything of which he has need'. We must learn to depend upon God – the God-ground of all that is – and not on ourselves. Which we can put into other words by saying that our true needs – intellectual, emotional and spiritual – will be looked after if we trust life and if we accept what it provides.

The 'faithful servant' might be said to be at that stage of growth, although perhaps not quite. His is the active path of good works and when Ruysbroeck was once asked what was the difference between the hireling and the faithful servant, he replied that it was all a matter of *intention*. The hireling obeys the commandments because he thinks it is in his best interests to do so, while the faithful servant does so for love of God, although he is still very much at the mercy of his own thoughts and feelings. Indeed even the faithful servant in Ruysbroeck's eyes was nowhere near so close to God as the inner friends of God, the third stage of growth; and one suspects from the slight acidity with which Ruysbroeck describes them, that he may have suffered from some of the faithful servants among his parishioners and fellow clergy. But he is also critical of those who are *too* inward, presumably those who spent all their time praying and meditating.

"We must now observe the great difference which there is between the faithful servants and the inward friends of God. For through grace and the help of God, the faithful servants have chosen to keep the commandments of God, that is, to be obedient to God and the Holy Church in all virtues and goodly behaviour: and this is called the outward or active life. But the inward friends of God choose to follow, besides the commandments, the quickening counsels of God, and this is a loving and inward cleaving to God for the sake of His eternal glory, with a willing abandonment of all that one may possess outside of God. . . . All such friends God calls and invites inwards, and He teaches them the distinctions of inward exercises and many a hidden way of ghostly [spiritual] life. But He sends His servants outwards, that they may be faithful to Him and to His house in every service and in every kind of good works.

"Behold, thus God gives His grace and His help to each man according to his fitness; that is, according to the way in which he is in tune with God, whether in outward good works or in the inward practice of love. But none can do and feel the inward exercises unless he be wholly turned inward to God. For as long as a man is divided of heart, so long as he looks outwards and is unstable of mind and is easily swayed by joy and grief in temporal things, for these are still alive within him . . . inwardly he abides in darkness, and knows not what inward exercises should be nor how these should be practised. But since he knows and feels that he has God in mind, and in all His works desires to fulfil His dearest will, with this it may be that he is content; for then he knows himself to be free from hypocrisy in his intention, and faithful in his service. And by these two things he contents himself; and it seems to him that outward good works done with a pure intention are more holy and more profitable than any inward exercise whatever, for by the help of God he has chosen an outward active way of virtue. And therefore he had rather exercise himself in the diversity of outward works than serve with inward love that same one for whom he works. And that is the cause why his mind is more filled with the works which he does, than with God, for whom he does them. And through this tendency to images in his works he remains an outward man and is not able to follow the counsels of God; for his exercise is more outward than inward, more of the senses than of the spirit. Though he is indeed a faithful servant of God in outward works, yet that which the secret friends of God experience remains hidden from and

27

unknown to him. And this is why certain gross and outward men always condemn and blame the inward and contemplative men, because they have in mind that these are idle.

"But there are also found some foolish men who would be so inward that they would neither act nor serve, even in those things of which their neighbour has need. Behold, these are neither secret friends nor faithful servants of God; but they are altogether false and deceived. For no man can follow the counsels of God who will not keep His commandments. And therefore all secret friends of God are also at the same time faithful servants wherever this is needful; but all the faithful servants are not secret friends for the exercise which belongs thereto is unknown to them."

Having penetratingly separated the sheep from the goats in this way, Ruysbroeck goes on to lay bare a more subtle distinction, which arises between the friends of God and His hidden sons, the final stage of growth. His most rhapsodic prose is reserved for the hidden sons and it is here that he brings us to the crux of the whole spiritual life – the difference between having God and being Him.

"But further we find a more subtle and inward difference between the secret friends and the hidden sons of God; and yet both these alike by their inward exercise maintain themselves in the presence of God. But the friends possess their inwardness as an attribute, for they choose the loving adherence to God as best and highest of all that they ever can and will reach: and that is why they cannot by themselves and their own activity penetrate to the imageless Nudity. For they have, as images and intermediaries between God and themselves, their own being and their own activity. And though in their loving adherence they feel united with God, yet, in this union they always feel a difference and an otherness between God and themselves. For the simple passing into the Bare and Wayless, they do not know and love: and therefore their highest inward life ever remains in Reason and in Ways. And though they have clear understanding and discernment of all the virtues that may be conceived, the simple staring with open heart into the Divine Brightness remains unknown to them. And though they feel themselves uplifted to God in a mighty fire of love, yet they keep something of their own selfhood, and are not consumed and burnt to nothingness in the unity of love. And though they may desire to live for ever more in the service of God and to please Him eternally, they will not die in God to all the selfhood of their spirit, and receive from Him a God-formed life. And even though they esteem little and count as nothing all consolation and all rest which may come from without, yet they greatly value the gifts of God and also their own inward works, and the solace and sweetness which they feel within; and thus they rest upon the way, and do not so wholly die to themselves as to be able to attain the highest beatitude in bare and wayless love. And even if they could practise and apprehend with clear discernment the perfection of loving adherence to God, and all the inward and upward going ways by which one may pass into the presence of God; yet the wayless passing, and the sublime wandering in the Superessential love, wherein neither end, nor beginning, nor way, nor manner, can ever be found, would remain hidden from and unknown of them.

"And so there is a great difference between the secret friends and the hidden sons of God. For the friends feel naught else but a loving and living ascent to God in some wise; but, above this, the sons experience a simple and death-like passing which is in no wise."

This 'death-like passing which is in no wise', or in no particular way, is the goal of all religions. It is the *moksha*, or liberation, of Hinduism, and the nirvana of Buddhism. It is the moment of utter and complete change from duality to oneness, when there is an inner integration so profound that the feeling of separate selfhood dies. The actual experience of this state may pass quite quickly or remain for some time, but it becomes increasingly apparent afterwards that one's actions are henceforth more balanced and spontaneous. They arise more from a sense of true beingness and less from an applied concept of what ought to be. For when we feel a separate selfhood we do our work consciously for the sake of God – or the Self, or the Dharma. But when we no longer feel that separateness our work becomes a spontaneous action of ourselves – 'one life with us', as Ruysbroeck says. In one of his most beautiful passages he describes the life of the sons of God.

"How may we become hidden sons of God and attain to the

God-seeing life? As to this I have apprehended the following. . . .In our approach to God, we must carry with us ourselves and all our works as a perpetual sacrifice to God; and in the presence of God, we must forsake all our works, and, dying in love, go forth from all creatureliness into the superessential richness of God: there we shall possess God in an eternal death to ourselves. . . . In the ordinary state of grace, when we are born of God into a ghostly and virtuous life, we carry our works before us as an offering to God; but in the wayless state, where we die back into God in an eternal and blessed life, there our good works follow us, for they are one life with us. When we go towards God by means of virtue, God dwells in us; but when we go out from ourselves and from all else, then we dwell in God. So soon as we have faith, hope and charity, we have received God, and He dwells in us with His grace, and He sends us out as His faithful servants to keep His commandments. And He calls us in again as His secret friends so soon as we are willing to follow his counsels; and He names us openly as His sons so soon as we live in opposition to the world. But if above all things we would taste God, and feel eternal life [timelessness] in ourselves, we must go forth into God with our feeling, above reason; and there we must abide, onefold, empty of ourselves, and free from images, lifted up by love into the simple bareness of our consciousness. For when we go out in love beyond and above all things, and die to all observation in ignorance and darkness, then we are wrought and transformed through the Eternal Word, Who is the Image of the Father. In this idleness of our spirit, we receive the Incomprehensible Light, which enwraps us and penetrates us, as the air is penetrated by the light of the sun. And this Light is nothing else than a fathomless staring and seeing. What we are, that we behold; and what we behold, that we are: for our thought, our life and our being are uplifted in simplicity, and made one with the Truth which is God. And therefore in this simple staring we are one life and one spirit with God: and this I call a contemplative life. As soon as we cleave to God we possess the better part; but when we gaze thus into our superessence, we possess God utterly. . . .

"This possession is a simple and abysmal tasting of all good and of eternal life; and in this tasting we are swallowed up above reason and without reason, in the deep quiet of the Godhead, which is never moved. That this is true we can only know by our own feeling, and in no other way. For how this is, or where, or what, neither reason nor practice can come to know: and therefore our ensuing exercise always remains wayless, that is, without manner. For that abysmal Good which we taste and possess, we can neither grasp nor understand; neither can we enter into it by ourselves or by means of our exercises. And so we are poor in ourselves, but rich in God; hungry and thirsty in ourselves, drunken and fulfilled in God; busy in ourselves, idle in God. And thus we shall remain throughout eternity. But without the exercise of love, we can never possess God; and whosoever thinks or feels otherwise is deceived. And thus we live wholly in God, where we possess our blessedness and we live wholly in ourselves, where we exercise ourselves in love towards God. And though we live wholly in God and wholly in ourselves, yet it is but one life. . . ."

Here Ruysbroeck has come to the second part of his teaching, which is that of man's relationship both to God and to the world. Living wholly in God and *at the same time* living wholly in ourselves was exactly how Ruysbroeck conceived it. "We cannot wholly become God and lose our created being, it is impossible," he says, "and if we remain wholly in ourselves, cut off from God, we should be miserable and unblest." So he came to see that it was necessary to live in the two states equally.

"Though I have said before that we are one with God, yet now I will say that we must eternally remain other than God, and distinct from Him. . . . And we must understand and feel both within us, if all is to be right with us."

Above all, Ruysbroeck was a practical mystic. He knew that if our ordinary everyday world is not properly Reality-centred, then we have missed the point altogether, however much we may read holy books or think mystical thoughts. So although it is essential to come to know that clear oneness of contemplation when the self is transcended, it is also *just as essential* to begin to live in the world in the best human way possible.

It is precisely at this vital point that medieval mysticism and

31

Zen Buddhism meet and merge. In his book *The Centre of Gravity* the Zen master, Joshu Sasaki, points out that there are two ways of being which we must come to know if we are to live properly. One way is to be unconditioned, when we experience the absence of 'me' – as for instance when the feeling of limited self is overcome by the beauty of sight or sound and there is *just* the moonlight on the sea, or the dappled shadows of trees, or the gentle sound of rain. Many westerners are unaware of this way of being, he says. The other way is when 'me' is there (our usual state) and 'me' and 'mine' are the predominant expressions of it. We have to learn, Sasaki says, to know both states, to become totally aware of them. We cannot and should not expect to stay in one state all the time because we are human beings, with all the limitations of mind and body that go with humanity. We are bound to alternate between the two states: but if we are conscious of both we are able to adjust the balance and to enter voluntarily into one state or the other. Without proper consciousness of it we can enter the unconditioned state, for instance, but then we can easily be knocked out of it by some interruption and cannot find it again. This is why Ruysbroeck himself says that 'we must understand and feel both within us, if all is to be right with us'.

In the West there is a strong tendency to gloss over or misunderstand the very nature of our humanity, particularly by those who are searching for transcendental states. We long so much for the God-ground that our conditioned humanity seems inferior and in some way separate from it. But the true mystic finds out that his humanity is totally acceptable and right. The very attempt to escape our humanness can lead us astray. Another of the strong links between medieval mysticism and northern Buddhism is the way in which both regard the world itself as sacred and the function of the human being to reflect its sacred nature.

Ruysbroeck, with a telling use of the word 'idle', by which he means inner stillness without thought, teaches the steps to be taken towards the God-ground and then, the goal reached, the inevitable and proper return to conditioned humanness.

"And therefore I say further: that from the face of God, or from our highest feeling, a brightness shines upon the face of our inward being, which teaches us the truth of love and of all virtues. . . . If, however, we would feel God within us, and have the fire of His love ever more burning within us, we must, of our own free will, help to kindle it in four ways: we must abide within ourselves, united with the fire through inwardness. And we must go forth from ourselves towards all men with loyalty and brotherly love. And we must go beneath ourselves in penance, betaking ourselves to good works, and resisting our inordinate lusts. And we must ascend above ourselves with the flame of this fire, through devotion and thanksgiving and praise, and fervent prayer, and must ever cleave to God with an upright intention and with sensible love. And thereby God continues to dwell in us with His grace; for in these four ways is comprehended every exercise which we can do with the reason, and in some wise, but without this exercise no one can please God. . . . And thus, in this first way, we feel God within us through His grace, if we wish to belong to Him.

"Secondly; when we possess the God-seeing life, we feel ourselves to be living *in* God; and from out of that life in which we feel God in ourselves, there shines forth upon the face of our inward being a brightness which enlightens our reason, and is an intermediary between ourselves and God. And if we with our enlightened reason abide within ourselves in this brightness, we feel that our created life incessantly immerses itself in its eternal life. But when we follow the brightness above reason with a simple sight, and with a willing leaning out of ourselves, toward our highest life, there we experience the transformation of our whole selves in God; and thereby we feel ourselves to be wholly enwrapped in God.

"And after this there follows the third way of feeling; namely, that we feel ourselves to be one *with* God; for, through the transformation in God, we feel ourselves to be swallowed up in the fathomless abyss of our eternal blessedness, wherein we can nevermore find any distinction between ourselves and God. And this is the highest feeling, which we cannot experience in any other way than in the immersion in love. And therefore, so soon as we are uplifted and drawn into our highest feeling, all our powers stand idle in an essential fruition; but our powers do not pass away into nothingness, for then we should lose our created being. And as long as we stand idle, with an inclined spirit, and with open eyes, but without reflection, so long we can contemplate and have fruition. But at the very moment when we seek to prove and to comprehend what it is that we feel, we fall back into reason, and there we find a distinction and an otherness between ourselves and God and find God outside ourselves in incomprehensibility.

"And hence the true way of distinction; which is that we feel God *and* ourselves. Here, at this moment, we now find ourselves living in the presence of God; and the truth which we receive from the face of God teaches us that God would be wholly ours and that He wills us to be wholly His."

In this way Ruysbroeck saw the possibility of man as 'deiform'. He would be 'ever at work and ever at rest', knowing at one and the same time the absolute and the relative. He would not leave active life but would make his activity perfect within his contemplation. Thus the two aspects of man's nature, when lived properly, would be but one living. Perhaps we can understand this better if we imagine that instead of our usual idea of two static states, one God and the other man, the reality of the God-ground is a mysterious dynamic wholeness which includes all aspects of ourselves. For we tend to regard God and man as being fixed in time and place, but if we sense them as the same *process*, then to be human is also to be one with the God-ground.

But to be deiform as Ruysbroeck conceived it is for most of us the work of a lifetime, and Ruysbroeck himself had times when he was far from deiform during his life in Brussels. While he was still a young man, probably in his thirties, he took on in verbal battle of a particularly strong and passionate nature, an older woman called Madame Bloemardinne, the head of one branch of the Brethren of the Free Spirit (see Introduction).

It was a strange and troubled time in Belgium. The artisans' revolt, which had been brutally smashed in 1306, had left a repressed bitterness and hatred which frequently erupted into bloodshed, keeping Brussels in a state of tension. Then large numbers of Beghards continually streamed into the capital from Germany, bringing with them unorthodox and 'heretical' beliefs. The people of Brussels violently sided with them against the Church, seeing them as witnesses to the true Gospel spirit in contrast to the pious veneer of the priests which covered up much corruption and degradation within the

Church. And no doubt most of the Beghards were filled with a simple desire to follow the path of Jesus, just as many of the 'flower people' of our own century genuinely believed that they were creating a new and truer style of life. But just as there were irresponsible hippies, content merely to drop out and do nothing, so there were Beghards who lived as pious tramps, begging everything and giving nothing.

The time was ripe then, with the power of the Church sapped from within by its own iniquities and from without by alternative beliefs, for a number of cults and sects to spring up. One of these, the Brethren of the Free Spirit, had itself split up since its early days into different and differing branches, one mainly ascetic and the other inclined to be freer, both in thought and morals. This freer branch believed that any urgent impulse was divine in nature, because all was divine. It was inspired and vitalised by Bloemardinne who, in the intensity of her nature, might be said to bear some resemblance to a medieval Madame Blavatsky.

The first appearance of this branch of the Brethren was at the beginning of the fourteenth century when they were known as Porrettistes after Marguerite Porrette, a Beguine. She had written a short book which contained the 'heretical' statement: "The soul that has annihilated itself in the love of the Creator can accord to nature everything it desires." For that sentiment she was burnt to death at Greve in 1310. But her doctrine did not die and it was taken up later by Bloemardinne, a rather mysterious figure. All we really know about her is that she sat on a silver throne when teaching or writing (her name is sometimes identified with that of a wealthy widow) and that two seraphim were reported to accompany her whenever she took holy communion. She wrote a good deal about seraphic love, taking Porrette's statement as freedom to follow all one's desires as long as one was in accord with God. She claimed supernatural powers, preached in favour of extreme quietism (never concerning oneself actively with the world), and generally created such a miasma of occult fascination that when she died hundreds of maimed and sick came to her bed, hoping to be healed by the touch of her body.

Such was Ruysbroeck's formidable female antagonist. Unfortunately his written words against her are lost and we only know through Pomerius that he made attacks on her in his sermons. In some ways it was not her personally whom Ruysbroeck detested but that which she represented and publicised. He saw her doctrine being taken to extremes by corrupt Brethren and followed by weak and foolish disciples.

What were his objections to a form of understanding which, while it was often silly and far from spiritual, yet helped to expand the minds of many? Even Pomerius could say: "I affirm from personal experience that the writings of Bloemardinne, although excessively baleful, have such an aspect of truth and piety that no one could perceive in them any seed of heresy. . . ."

Perhaps that is the clue we are looking for. Pomerius could see no heresy, but Ruysbroeck, with a clearer idea of the spiritual life, did perceive it; and perhaps the line between truth and error was so narrow that many could not perceive it and therefore Ruysbroeck had to fling himself into a passionate defence of what he considered the right view in order to convince anybody. Yet it remains a curious episode in his life, for even he said that there were not many Brethren who went to sinful extremes.

Whether it was Bloemardinne's esoteric and magnetic renderings of the scriptures, or her doctrine itself which seemed to him harmful, there is no doubt that this was the one time in Ruysbroeck's peaceful life when he was blazingly angry. His fury was probably first set alight by episodes of serious cruelty to the Jews, whom the people looked upon as responsible for all the tension and trouble caused by the open opposition of the Beghards and Lollards to the ecclesiastical authorities. As a boy Ruysbroeck must have known of the massacre of the Jews in 1308; he was a man when the scene was repeated in 1315 – at that time because of the high price of food consequent on a cattle plague.

There can be no doubt that the brutal, dehumanising cruelty of these events had a deep effect on Ruysbroeck. He made a connection between the whole disturbed scene of Brussels and the spirit of 'do what you will' among Bloemardinne's followers – indeed the whole spirit of religious individualism which was anti-sacrament, anti-tradition and anti-authority. When he saw the converts Bloemardinne was making he attacked her from the pulpit and unmasked her writings without troubling about the enemies he might make for himself. Sides were taken throughout Brussels. Songs were made up about Ruysbroeck and people ridiculed him in the street. Unfortunately Bloemardinne's pamphlets and Ruysbroeck's refutations have never been found and it is thought that Ruysbroeck may have destroyed the lot. But he wrote his first book as a result of the dispute and all his opinions are encapsulated there. Bloemardinne had had the wit to circulate her writings in the native tongue rather than in Latin. Ruysbroeck decided to do the same but to create a positive and constructive book of true mysticism rather than a merely negative denial of what the Brethren believed in. So *The Book of the Kingdom of God's Lovers* was born, but Ruysbroeck was not pleased with it and only allowed it to be published at a later date. Eventually it was superseded by *The Adornment of the Spiritual Marriage*, his major work, probably written in 1335.

In both these books there is nevertheless a strong refutation against false mystics. The books denounce what Ruysbroeck found particularly offensive in their doctrine. One fault was their lack of humility which led them to the assumption that they were God, *in the wrong sort of way*. He quotes this as one of their assumptions: "While I was in my eternal essence, I had no God. But that which I was I willed, and that which I willed, I was. It is of my own will that I have become. . . . Without me, God would have neither knowledge nor will-power, for it is I, with God, who have created my own personality and all things. From my hand are suspended heaven, earth and all creatures. And whatever honour is paid to God, it is to me that it is paid, for in my essential being I am by nature God. For myself, I neither hope nor love, and I have no faith, no confidence in God. I have nothing to pray for, nothing to implore, for I do not render honour to God above myself. For in God there is no distinction, neither Father nor Son nor Holy Spirit. . . . With this God I am one, and am even that which He is . . . and which, without me, He is not."

Such a statement certainly might make the blood boil of anyone who took it seriously. By saying they were God the Brethren distorted the true mystical apprehension of God in which there can be no such assertions. Martin Buber, a Hebrew mystic of this century, once pointed out that the 'person' experiences unconditioned Reality, but the ego becomes the conditioned self-conscious 'me'.

"The person says 'I am'; the ego says, 'That is how I am'. 'Know thyself' means to the person: know yourself as being. To the ego it means: know your being-that-way."

The Brethren were undoubtedly confusing these two states and believing that any act of the ego, however futile and depraved, was God's action and therefore right; while Ruysbroeck, with his greater understanding, could not bear such distortion.

"They are", he says in *The Book of Truth*, "a fruit of hell, the more dangerous because they counterfeit the true fruit of the Spirit of God."

He goes on to say that the soul's reaction to the experience of the Infinite must inevitably be one of humility, whereas the 'pantheists' are full of conceit and self-satisfaction. And "they believe themselves sunk in inward peace; but as a matter of fact they are deep-drowned in error".

This last objection (to them as quietists) was perhaps Ruysbroeck's strongest one. He loathed the laziness and lack of self-discipline and effort which led them to sit or lie about 'in contemplation'. He described it as "consisting in nothing but an idleness and interior vacancy, to which they are inclined by nature and habit".

Again one is reminded of parallels in other religions. When Dogen, a thirteenth-century Japanese Buddhist, went to China to study under the great Ch'an master, Ju Ching, he was told to practise zazen (sitting meditation) constantly. He fell into the 'quietist' error of sitting vacantly, waiting for some sort of enlightenment to take place, until one day he heard the master, who was making his early round of inspection, scolding another monk because he was dozing. The master said: "The practice of zazen is the dropping away of body and mind. What do you think dozing is going to accomplish?" When he overheard these words Dogen suddenly saw that zazen was not a mere sitting still: it was the dynamic opening up of the self to its own reality, by letting go of all ideas about life.

In the same way, the master Ruysbroeck must have felt that such true intensity of effort was lacking in the Brethren. "If", he said, "their nature is prone to that which gives it satisfaction, and if in realising it mental idleness must, however slightly, be either checked or distracted, they obey the instincts of nature."

Perhaps Ruysbroeck devoted too much time to denunciation. Such a frame of mind, however, was well and truly vanquished when he came to the most luminous, mystical and joyous part of his life. He was fifty. It was then that the three companions decided to quit the noisy Brussels life and retreat to a forest hermitage.

Life for all three had been hard in Brussels. Respect for the Church was at such a low ebb that its priests were often treated with ridicule. Church services were noisy with bickering and loud conversations, and sermons were often interrupted by the argumentative. "When you sin and say vulgar words and nobody corrects *you*," said one voice to a preacher, "then the people have a saying: 'Let God and me alone!'"

Even the clergy were divided against each other and it was not unknown for the church to be the scene of drunken brawls between them. In this atmosphere the three friends struggled against hostility, ignorance and stupidity. And then came the last straw, perhaps the final determining factor which led them away from Brussels to the forest. Van Coudenberg was accused of treason, of accepting bribes from the King of France. Although he was never convicted his name appeared on the banishment lists signed by Jean III after the failure of the siege of Tournai (1340) and he was compelled to leave the city.

It was through van Coudenberg's influence with the Duke of Brabant that the three found their sanctuary. The Duke gave them the old hermitage of Groenendael (green valley) in the forest of Soignes, not far from Brussels. It was ideal for their purpose for the forest had long been a home for hermits and anchorites. Seven beautiful lakes, as well as the great silent forest glades, made Groenendael a refuge of indescribable peace and beauty.

For the first five years the three lived there as they were, bound by no other rule than their own spirit of prayer and contemplation. But as time went on and news of their serene and saintly state grew, they began to be besieged by pilgrims and penitents. Many wanted to join them in the forest, yet others flocked from Brussels for spiritual help and consolation. And even more distracting was a constant coming and going of huntsmen from the château of Brabant. The forest was a favourite ground for the chase and the hermitage itself seemed a convenient meeting place for rest and refreshment. The continual parties of noisy men and dogs, as well as pleasure parties from the town, put a great strain on the hospitality of the hermitage, but it would not have been wise to complain to the Duke; nor could they claim any cloister privileges since they were not established as a regular community.

So point and force was given to a request from Paris that they should regularise their status. The Church was not at all in favour of communities living outside the known monastic orders. The three decided to conform. They asked to become Augustinian canons and permission was immediately granted. The Priory of Groenendael was formally founded with van Coudenberg as its provost and Ruysbroeck as its prior. Sadly, Hinckaert, now a very old man and in poor health, felt that he would not be up to the rigour of the austere rule; and rather than be a hindrance to the small community he did not take the vows. Instead a cell was built just outside the cloister and there he lived peacefully until his death.

As Prior of Groenendael, Ruysbroeck at last came into his own. Now there was time for contemplation and for that inner realisation of the God-ground which must have been so hard to practise in Brussels. The natural life of the forest about him created a particular harmony in Ruysbroeck and his fame soon spread as one who was both saintly and illumined. But his own good sense of humility prevented him from ever seeking dispensation from any task that needed to be done, in spite of the constant demands on his time, and he took his turn at everything, including heavy manual labour.

Ruysbroeck was to spend thirty-eight years at Groenendael, undoubtedly the most serene and happy of his life. He believed that all the books he wrote then were directly inspired by the Holy Ghost and he had a favourite tree in the forest under which he would receive these teachings and write them down. One of the most famous stories about him is concerned with this tree. One day he was gone such a long time that some brothers went in search of him. They found him still sitting beneath the tree writing, but surrounded by light as though the branches were aflame. The memory of this miracle was never lost in the community and for generations the tree was known and venerated as Ruysbroeck's Tree. The story led to the traditional representation of him – sitting under the tree, a stylus in his hand and a tablet on his knee, while both he and tree are encircled in brilliant rays of light.

His teaching became very simple. One day two young priests arrived from Brussels, wanting to know how they could increase their spirituality. Ruysbroeck gave them their answer in one all-embracing, profound sentence: "You are as holy as you wish to be." The priests were out of their depth with such simplicity – no doubt they had expected a long and complicated sermon. They suspected Ruysbroeck of sarcasm, complained to the canons in Brussels, and generally built up the whole incident preposterously. When they heard of this, some of Ruysbroeck's community brought the priests back and asked Ruysbroeck to explain his meaning. "But is it not simple?" he asked. "Is it not true? You are just as holy as you want to be. Your good will is the measure of your spirit. Look into yourselves and see what good will you have, and you will also see the standard of your holiness." The priests were satisfied.

On another occasion, a woman sent for Ruysbroeck, begging him to visit her. She was in a great state, believing that God had abandoned her because her health was so bad that she had no strength with which to perform acts of mercy, and physical suffering took away all her taste for prayer. What was she to do? "You can do nothing more pleasing to God, my dear child," replied Ruysbroeck, "than simply and utterly to accept His holy will. Try to give up your own desires and give Him thanks for all the things that are."

Perhaps some people believed his answers to be too glib. Gerard Groot, who was to become his disciple and the great friend of his old age, reproved him at their first meeting for the boundless confidence he seemed to have in the mercy of God – a confidence which, thought Groot, tasted of arrogance and presumption. He quoted to Ruysbroeck some of the most terrifying passages from the Bible about penalties for the wicked. Ruysbroeck replied serenely, "I assure you that you have failed to inspire me with fear. I am ready to accept whatever is destined for me in life or in death. I can conceive of nothing better, nothing safer, nothing more sweet. All my desires are restricted to this – that God may ever find me ready to do what He asks of me."

In Ruysbroeck's eyes, the greatest virtue, the one which would lead directly to the apprehension of the God-ground, was humility. He prized it above all others (as did St Bernard) seeing it as growing directly out of self-awareness. The more one is aware of one's own beingness, the more one is also aware of how infinite and mysterious that beingness is, and such awareness brings about true humbleness. With self-knowledge there comes perspective, the space to see things as they are, and the discovery of one's proper place in existence. Ruysbroeck called this understanding 'the solid foundation of the kingdom of the soul'. In our own time, the balance of the personality which arises from such self-awareness has been likened to the little figures which are so weighted that they cannot tip over. The unity of the self becomes such that whatever conditions it meets it will not lose its centre: "So the man goes out, and knows and finds himself through this simple light which has been poured into him, to be united and established and penetrated and confirmed, in the unity of his spirit and mind. Thereby the man is raised up and set in a new state, and he turns inwards and fixes his memory upon the Nudity, above all the distractions of sensible images, and above multiplicity. Here the man possesses the essential and supernatural unity of his spirit as his own dwelling-place and as his own eternal, personal heritage."

Ruysbroeck died at the age of eighty-eight, peacefully and joyfully. He had started a tradition in his lifetime of a certain kind of mystical apprehension, one which saw God and man as one whole and living process. This tradition was to be continued by Gerard Groot and by his disciple, Thomas à Kempis, the author of *The Imitation of Christ*.

Looking at Ruysbroeck's life from our far viewpoint, perhaps the most striking thing is not his distance from us but his nearness. His 'peaceful and joyous countenance, his humble good-natured speech' come clearly to us and are not veiled by his evident human weaknesses. In his own person he lived as truly as he could the 'deified man'; breathing in, as he put it, the love of God and breathing out that same love towards all creatures. "To give and receive both at once is the essence of union" he said. His retreat to Groenendael and the amount of writing he did there never kept him from anyone who asked for his help. We see him living up to his own ideal of the 'really humble man, without any pose or pretence', and we also see someone who gave up, to the best of his ability, everything in life that was not centred in God.

He was not a theologian. He was learned enough but he was too straightforward a man to speak of anything but that which mattered to him most and which he himself knew inwardly. It was characteristic of him that when asked to give a sermon he would sometimes admit that he had nothing to say. In the solitude of the forest his character became more and more simplified and integrated until he arrived at the 'God-seeing' stage, when he found Reality in everything.

To him this was the experience of the God-ground as both transcendent and immanent, both infinite and here and now. "To know yourself is to forget yourself," said Dogen, "and to forget yourself is to be enlightened by everything in the world." Ruysbroeck came to 'know' or to 'be' himself, his true self, centred in the God-ground. And when he truly 'was', all that he then saw also 'was'.

In spite of attacks by the Church for his 'pantheism', he remained utterly loyal, believing that what he taught was true Christianity and eventually convincing the authorities of this. "The language of God is found essentially and personally in all mankind" he wrote. "Each possesses it whole, entire and undivided. . . . God in the depths of us receives God who comes to us; it is God contemplating God. . . . He enters, but this was already his abode; wherein he dwells, there he enters in. Wherein he comes, therein he was already dwelling, for he never goes forth from himself. He knows neither chance nor change. Thus does the spirit possess God in the nudity of its substance, and God the spirit; it lives in God and God in it."

And (which helped him with the Church) he likened this action to the Holy Trinity: "[The soul] is like an eternal and living mirror of God, continually and uninterruptedly receiving the eternal begetting of the Son. . . . Hence it comes about that the substance of our soul possesses three properties which form but one in nature. The first property of the soul is an essential imageless bareness: through this we resemble and are one with the Father and his divine nature. The second property may be called the higher reason of the soul: it is a mirror-like clearness wherein we receive the Son of God, eternal truth. By reason of this clearness we are like him. The third property we call the spark of the soul: it is an intimate and natural tendency of the soul towards its source, and it is there that we receive the Holy Spirit."

It is possible to misunderstand such teaching and to believe that the whole personality is to be obliterated before Reality can be known. Ruysbroeck did not mean this at all. Our individuality, he said, is the pattern by which we know Reality, and as we learn to drop the false images and veils which hide us from ourselves, so our individual personality or pattern emerges clearly. Then we see with 'a simple eye' and all our attributes of love and will and thought begin their journey inwards, moving away from superficial levels of speculation and desire and turning evermore towards that intrinsic God-ground which, like a magnet, pulls us towards itself. When we make that journey towards 'God in the depths of us', Ruysbroeck said, we enter into a new state of consciousness which he called 'the vision of God beyond and above reason'.

How to begin this journey? Essentially it is made through contemplation and then expressed in action, like the continual ebb and flow of the sea. But contemplation comes first:

> Contemplation is a knowing without mode,
> Forever abiding above the reason.
> Never can it descend therein,
> And above it reason can never ascend.
> The shining forth of That which has no mode is
>   as a fair mirror,
> Wherein there shines the everlasting light of God.
> It is without attributes,
> And therein all the workings of reason fail.
> It is not God;
> But it is that light whereby we see him.
> They who walk in the divine light thereof,
> Discover in themselves the Unconfined.

That which has no mode is above reason, not
    without it;
And it perceives all things without curiosity.
Curiosity is far beneath it,
And the life of contemplation is without curiosity.
That which has no mode sees, but knows not what
    is seen,
Since it is above all, and is neither This nor That.
                    (Ruysbroeck, *The Twelve Beguines*)

Julian of Norwich

Julian stands on her own among mystics. She has a particular basic honesty, a tough tenacity to search out answers to her questions, and at the same time a remarkably comfortable friendly sweetness. She talks straight to her reader as she must have talked to her friends and visitors, describing God 'who is unmade' and the Trinity in simple, homely style, because the things which she had seen, heard and felt were so convincing as to be objective truth to her, about which she wanted to talk freely. She was not in the least credulous – but certain unusual things happened to her which she observed with the greatest precision and attention (and occasionally with doubt as well) and these experiences were the means by which she came to understand the Reality of her life.

Julian is thought by some to be the greatest of the English mystics since her remarkable and mysterious revelations were equalled by her thoughtful, contemplative understanding of them. She received bodily visions and intellectual visions of Christ and the Trinity and through these she developed an intuitive penetration into many of the perplexities of Christianity and indeed of all religion. Her revelations equalled those of St Theresa of Avila and, like St Theresa, although her writing is completely personal she is altogether objective about the experiences themselves. Yet her account is no mere catalogue of interesting states. It is a full theology in itself and gives us the deeply-considered responses to awe-inspiring visions of a woman who was above all sane, as well as being highly intelligent, wise and open-minded.

Her theology is concerned with the all-embracingness of divine love, both received and given. In the light of this love, which to her was ultimate Reality, every problem became unimportant and she saw all created things in a new dimension. She saw that the nature of the world and of the individual is as nothing compared to the infinity and timelessness of the God-ground; yet in another sense all is infinitely precious since it originates from and is sustained by that Reality itself. "He is our clothing that, for love, wraps us up and winds us about; embraces us, all encloses us and hangs about us, for tender love; so that he can never leave us."

Her whole theology rings with positive assurance – with joy and happiness in the unique fact that she and all beings are created at all. She sees in our very existence the amazing opportunity we are given to transcend the insignificant and to become that which is the whole meaning of our lives. To her this That was God the Father – for she was properly a woman of her century and thoroughly entrenched in the religious tradition and language of her age (although often she gladdens us with not so much a Catholic interpretation as an unlabelled and timeless one) – and every creature who could begin to feel a new beingness was the Father's 'courteous' gift to his Son; "for we are his bliss, we are his prize, we are his worship, we are his crown".

About her life little is known since she herself did not consider her outward circumstances important and barely refers to them. It is known from accounts about her, however, that she was an anchoress – a hermit living in a cell built on to the wall of a church in Norwich – and that she was born about 1343. Her anchorage was destroyed in the sixteenth century but the foundations remain. The church too was destroyed in the Second World War, but a chapel and shrine were reconstructed and dedicated to her in 1953. We know that she lived to a good age, for Margery Kempe, a minor mystic in her own right, visited Julian in 1413 and received excellent advice from the still active old woman.

Her cell would have had at least two windows. One of these opened on to the church, so that she could take part in all services; and the other opened on to the outside world. People who wanted advice or consolation would come to this outside window and thus she kept in touch with the life of the town. When she was in meditation and not to be disturbed, a curtain embroidered with a cross would be drawn over the window. That she had plenty of visitors is not to be doubted. Norwich was second in size only to London at that time and there were

Flemish weavers who moved to and fro between Belgium and East Anglia, as well as the teaching friars who would undoubtedly discuss religious matters with her when their journeys brought them to Norwich; and there were all the people of the town.

Properly we should speak of her as 'the Lady Julian' for that would have been her title since she was a *Domna*, as were the Benedictine nuns of Carrow, to which her anchorage probably belonged. But since in all her relationships she was tender and motherly, it seems more natural to call her 'Mother Julian', and almost certainly this was the title by which many knew her.

It is likely that Julian was a gentlewoman of some education, although in one of her books she calls herself unlettered. However, she wrote two books of a uniquely beautiful and individual type and the learning they show does not seem to belong to an illiterate background. Until fairly recently the longer book, *The Revelations of Divine Love*, was thought to be merely an extension of the shorter one, *The Showings of Divine Love*. But it is now believed that *The Showings* was written at the time or immediately after the events it describes, whereas *The Revelations* was written some twenty years later and contains all her understanding of those events, arrived at through meditation, contemplation and further insight. She was remarkably observant, as a trained scientist might be, determined to present the occasion with detailed accuracy to such a degree that even when she and all those about her believed her close to death she was still able to note clearly the reactions of the priest who gave her the last sacraments.

The only fragment of historical autobiography she allows us is at the start of the second chapter of *The Revelations*: "These revelations were showed to a simple unlearned creature living in this mortal flesh, in the year of our Lord one thousand, three hundred and seventy-three, on the thirteenth day of May." In the same lucid and dispassionate style, one which wanted above all to draw attention away from herself so that all could be centred on God, she refers to herself as a 'creature': "before this time the creature desired three gifts from God. The first was understanding of the Passion; the second was bodily sickness at thirty years of age; the third was to have by God's gift three wounds."

She explains exactly what she meant by this:

"For the first grace I thought I had a great feeling for the Passion of Christ but I longed to have yet more, by God's gift. I wished I had been there at that time, with Mary Magdalen and others who were Christ's lovers, that I might have seen with bodily eyes the passion that our Lord suffered for me – and suffered with him, as others did who loved him. . . . Other sight or showing of God desired I never none until my soul should be gone from my body . . . my meaning was that if I were given to know the bodily pains of our Lord and the compassion of our Lady and of all the true lovers who were living at that time and saw his pains – for I would have been one of them and suffered with them – I should afterwards have more true understanding of the Passion.

"For the second grace: it came into my mind freely, without any seeking, a longing desire to have of God's gift a bodily sickness. I wanted that this sickness should be grievous to the point of death with I myself believing that I should die, and every other creature that saw me thinking the same. For I wished to have no comfort in earthly living. In this sickness I wanted to have all manner of pains, bodily and mental, that I should have were I to have died – all save the actual departing of the soul. I hoped that it might be a help to me when I did come to die, for I longed to be with God soon.

"These two desires, the passion and the sickness, I wanted with a condition attached; for I believed that this was not an ordinary prayer. So I said: 'Lord, you know what I want, if it is your will that I should have it; and if it is not your will, good Lord, be not displeased with me, for I will only as you will.' This sickness – which I thought of in my youth – I desired to have when I was thirty years of age.

"For the third grace: I heard a priest telling the story of St Cecilia and how she received three wounds from a sword in the neck, from which she pined to death. I was so moved that I conceived a mighty desire that God would grant me three wounds in my lifetime, these the wound of repentance, the wound of compassion and the wound of great longing for God. And just as I asked for the other two with a condition, so I asked for the third with no condition at all."

Never, surely, were three wishes so strange as these – to see

Jesus in agony on the cross; to develop a sickness leading to near-death; and to receive three wounds to the spirit. Such intense and death-lingering longings belong to adolescence and it is surely Julian as a young girl – 'which I thought of in my youth' – who prayed for them and who probably pictured thirty as being a long way off. For she tells us: "The first two desires passed from my mind, but the third dwelt with me all the time." In order to forget two such unusual desires, so that they passed right out of her mind, a good deal of time must have elapsed before they were realised.

For Julian's three wishes came true. In proper karmic style, she developed a seemingly fatal illness when she was thirty, becoming paralysed first in the lower half of the body and then in the upper, so that her eyes were fixed and her breath giving out. She believed herself on the point of death and received the last rites of the Church. Then her illness, having lasted for five or six days, suddenly left her and: "I felt as whole again as ever I was before or after, especially in the upper part of the body. I marvelled at this sudden change and thought that it must be a secret working of God and not of nature. And yet I did not trust that I would live because of feeling easier; and the feeling of this ease was no true ease to me. For I thought I would rather have been free of this world – my heart was set on that."

It was then that the other desire came into her mind – to share the suffering of Jesus as though she were both feeling the pain and at the same time extending all her compassion towards that pain. She is careful to tell us that she never actually asked for a 'bodily sight' or any other revelations from God, but only for compassion "such as a kind soul might have towards our Lord Jesus, who willed for love to become a mortal man".

Beyond all her expectations, however, she found, while concentrating on the cross held up to her in her illness, that she was gazing at "the red blood running down from under the garland of thorns, hot and fresh, plentiful and lifelike, just as I thought it must have been at that time when the garland was thrust down onto his blessed head . . . it came to me truly that it was God himself that showed it me without any intermediary, and then I said, 'Lord bless us!' in a mighty voice and meaning great reverence. For greatly was I astonished by the wonder and marvel that he who is so reverenced would be so homely with a sinful creature still alive in her mortal flesh.

"At the same time that I saw this bodily sight of his bleeding head, our Lord showed me ... a little thing, the size of a hazelnut, which seemed to lie in the palm of my hand, and it was as round as any ball. I looked at it and thought, 'What may this be?' and I was answered in a general way, thus: 'It is all that is made.' I wondered how long it could last for I thought it might fall suddenly to nothing, it was so little. And the answer came to my understanding, 'It lasts and always shall last because God loves it, and just in this way everything has its being – through the love of God.'

"In this little thing I saw three parts. The first is that God made it, the second that God loves it, and the third that he sustains it. And what did I find in this? Truly, the maker, the lover and the sustainer. And until I am oned to him in myself I can never have full rest nor true bliss; that is to say, until I am so fastened to him that there is no created thing at all between my God and me. And this little thing that is made – seeming as though it would fade away to nothing, it was so small – we need to have knowledge of this. We should take as nothing everything that is made, so that we can love and have God who is unmade. For this is the reason why we are not at ease in heart or soul: that we seek here rest in this thing that is so little, where no rest can be, and are unknowing of our God who is very rest. He wills us to know him and he likes that we rest in him. All that is below cannot be sufficient for us. And this is the reason why no soul can be at rest until it is naughted of everything that is made. When the soul is willingly made naught for love, so as to have him who is all, then she will be in real rest.

"And also our good Lord showed that it is full great pleasure to him that a simple soul should come to him nakedly, plainly and homely. This is the yearning of the soul when it is touched by God, as I have understood by this showing.

"God of your goodness give me yourself, for you are enough for me and I can ask for nothing else than full worship of you. And if I ask for anything that is less, I shall always want; for only in you have I everything."

In all, Julian had sixteen different 'showings'. Even while she

51

held the little thing the size of a hazelnut in her hand she was continuing to watch "the great drops of blood which fell from under the garland like pellets, seeming to come out of the veins; and in coming out they were reddish-brown and the blood was full thick; but in spreading forth they were bright red. And when they came to the eyebrows there they vanished.

"And the bleeding went on until many things were seen and understood. Yet still the beauty and lifelikeness continued in the same way. And the plentifulness of the blood was like to the drops of water that fall out of the eaves of a house after a great shower of rain, when they fall so quickly that no man can number them. And in their roundness they were like to the scales of a herring. These three likenesses came into my mind at the time: pellets for the roundness of the drops as they came out; scales of herring for their roundness as they spread; raindrops from the eaves of a house for the innumerable plenteousness.

"This showing was vivid and lifelike and hideous and dreadful and sweet and lovely. But of all the sights that I saw, this was the greatest comfort to me: that our good Lord, who is so reverend and dreadful is also so homely and courteous. And this filled me full of liking and sureness in soul."

This last thought is one on which she dwells with affectionate frequency. She saw God as being so homely and considerate that he enveloped everything with his love, even down to the most intimate bodily functions – "Man goes upright; his food is taken and hidden in his body as in a very fine purse. And when it is necessary the purse is opened, and then it is shut again – all in seemly fashion. That it is God that works this is shown where it is said: 'He comes down to us, to the lowest part of our need.' For he despises nothing which he has made. And he does not disdain to serve us in the simplest offices that belong to nature and to our body, for the love of our soul that is made in his own likeness. For as the body is clad in clothes, and the flesh in skin, and the bones in flesh, and the heart in the breast; so are we, body and soul, clad and enclosed in the goodness of God."

In this way Julian easily solved the problem of duality, of the spirit versus the flesh – a problem which has bedevilled much of Christianity. She saw quite clearly that everything is created, that nothing can be left out. That which is, is God. And this deeply intimate belonging was more joyful to her than if God had bestowed great gifts but yet had remained remote and strange to her.

When this first powerful showing of Christ's blood came to a stop and faded away, she was still under the impression that she was dying and thought that the vision must have been meant for those who would still be alive. She wanted to share it quickly with her 'even-Christians' – "that they might all see and know the same as I saw, for I would like it to be a comfort to them".

She stops, however, in her narrative to warn her readers not to pay attention to "the poor wretch that it was showed to", but to God, "who, of his courteous love and endless goodness wanted to show it generally for the comfort of us all. For it is God's will that you accept it with as great a joy and delight as if Jesus had showed it to you all."

In her clear-sighted way, she also wanted it known that such a showing *of itself* did not make her a better person. "I am not good because of the showing, but only if I love God the better for it. For truly it was not showed to me that God loved me better than any soul who is least in grace. And I am sure that there are many who never have showing nor sight except from the ordinary teaching of the Church, who love God better than I."

Her second showing followed quickly on the first for she longed to continue to see things 'bodily'. But what was given was only partial – "a spitting, soiling and buffeting and many distressing pains, more than I can describe, and often a change of colour. At one time I saw half the face, from the ear, covered with dry blood to the centre of the face; and after that the other half, covered in the same way. This I saw bodily but murkily and darkly and I desired more bodily light to see more clearly."

She doubted in fact if such a dim vision – 'so low, so little and so simple' – was a real showing at all. "And I was answered in my mind: 'If God wills to show you more, he shall be your light, you need none but him.'"

Her third showing was not bodily but in her mind. She herself analysed her visions into three categories: "by bodily sight, by words formed in my understanding and by ghostly

sight [mental image]". The third showing was in her understanding and she saw God as a point.

"By which I saw that he is in all things. I gazed attentively,
perceiving and knowing in that understanding that he does all
that is done. With a soft marvel and dread, I thought, 'Then
what is sin?' For I saw truly that God does all things be they
never so small. And I saw that nothing is done by mere chance,
but all by the timeless foreseeing wisdom of God. If a thing
seems to be by chance according to man's judgement, it is
because of our own blindness and lack of knowledge. For those
things that exist in the wise foreseeing of God from without-
beginning, which he rightly and continually brings to their best
conclusion – when they happen they seem to come to our
notice suddenly and without our expecting them. And so
because of our blindness and lack of knowledge we say that
these things are by chance. But I understood in this showing of
love, and know truly, that in what God does there is no chance.
Therefore I must grant that all that is done is well done, since
God does it all."

How beautifully Julian handles the whole mystery of our
lives! From a 'without-beginning' things exist; and their
existence is beyond our comprehension. But in our arrogant
ignorance we deny their mystery and bestow on them a cause –
chance. By doing this we place ourselves in a nightmare world
of insecurity where chance can knock us down any day, and
even if it raises us high we never know when we will fall. But to
take the correct view, says Julian, we must see that what
happens has its own reasons, which we can never know. We
must trust that we are being looked after and that this
moment, with whatever it brings, is the right moment for us.

She goes on to say: "He is the mid-point of all things, and he
does all; but I was sure that he does no sin. Then I saw truly
that sin is a no-deed; for in all this sin was not showed to me.
Nor would I any longer wonder about this, but simply behold
our Lord and what he willed to show me.

How sensible! Sin is a 'no-deed' – not a positive thing but a
deficiency, a lack of understanding and of good. And instead of
endless speculations about the nature of sin and how God can
allow it to exist, she refuses to worry but simply 'beholds our
Lord' and trusts absolutely in her beholding. Doing this, she

soars above the theologians who are obsessed with the itch to interpret, to find meaning. She understood that if we discover the Reality of our life, there is no longer any need to make sense out of things or to interpret them. They simply are and each instant is a new seeing. The longing to analyse and to attach labels is a merely human occupation, leading nowhere ultimate, revealing nothing absolute, and merely blurring the impact of the here and now with a fog of doubt and speculation. That which is, is.

Julian was frankly surprised by the verdict on sin, particularly since it did not really agree with the teaching of the Church. To begin with she solved the dilemma with typical warm wisdom by pointing out that sin can be transmuted and made the means of man's awakening. She saw that sin has a dynamic quality which lends itself to transformation into its opposite – whereas mindless inertia, a disease from which we suffer a good deal today, is a far graver problem and much more likely to wreck the world.

"God showed that sin shall be no shame but rather worship to man. For just as with every sin there is a corresponding pain, so for every sin there is given bliss to the same soul by love . . . sin is the sharpest scourge that any soul can be smitten with – a scourge which greatly affects a man or woman, breaking him in pieces and purging him of all his self-love so much that sometimes he thinks himself fit only to sink in hell; until such time as he is touched by the Holy Ghost and remorse overtakes him, turning his bitterness into hope and love of God. When he has suffered sorrow and shame he will be healed and rewarded by the courteous love of God . . . who sees sin as sorrow and pain to his lovers; and to them he assigns no blame, for love."

She adds: "By repenting we are made clean, by compassion we are made ready, and by true longing for God we are made worthy . . . it is by these medicines that every sinful soul must be healed."

Julian saw God as all-forgiving – not from outside but from within ourselves so that our self-hatred is transformed into self-compassion, into a tender and loving transmutation of all our faults. She was delighted that 'God assigns no blame, for love'. She could see for herself that saints are ordinary human beings who have often made mistakes and committed sins and yet whose transformed imperfections have become 'not wounds but honours'.

"My understanding was lifted up into heaven," she said, "and God brought joyfully into my mind David and others in the old Testament without number. And in the new Testament he brought first Magdalen, then Peter and Paul, Thomas and Jude. . . ." As Underhill remarks, 'it was a great joy to Julian to feel that heaven was as wide and tolerant as her own heart'.

Yet she never viewed sin in any feeble or sentimental way. She saw 'fiends' – and in that she was truly medieval, for it was a fashion of that age – and yet her personality was so original that she could use her sense of humour even over the Devil.

"After this the fiend came again with his heat and with his stench, and made me full restless. . . . Also I heard a bodily jangling and speaking as if it had been of two people (and both, to my thinking, jangled at once, with great earnestness, as though they were holding a *parliament*); all was soft muttering and I did not understand what they were saying. . . ."

Yet she did not underestimate the power of evil. "Our failing is dreadful, our falling is shameful, and our dying is sorrowful. But in all this the sweet eye of pity and love never comes off us, nor does the working of mercy ever cease."

She could not help seeing the working of love and compassion even in the most appalling situations, yet in case she painted too pleasant a picture of the joys awaiting the reformed sinner, she added a warning:

"If now, because of all this comfort I have mentioned, any person is foolishly tempted to think that it must be good to sin in order to get a better reward – then let them beware of this temptation. For truly it is false. For the same true love that touches us all with its blessed strengthening, this same blessed love teaches us to hate sin, for the sake of love."

How true this is. There is no power like the power of selfless love to make sinning seem stupid and abhorrent. Humanist reasoning, ethical prohibitions – none have the deep effect of compassionate love. "Love and do what you will" said St Augustine, knowing full well that if you truly love you will do what is right.

Nevertheless the problem of sin still troubled Julian and

later in her life unease overtook her when she had to acknowledge that what she spoke of was not the teaching of the Church. So she thought it out and reconciled the distinction between the open condemnation of sin practised by the Church and her conviction that beyond this teaching there is something which has never been revealed.

"At one time our good Lord said: 'All things shall be well'; and at another he said: 'You shall see for yourself that all manner of thing shall be well.' In these two sayings were various levels of understanding. One was this: he wants us to know that he takes heed not only of noble things and great, but also of little and small, low and simple – of both the one and the other. This is his meaning when he says: 'all manner of thing shall be well', for he wants us to know that the least thing shall not be forgotten. Another understanding was this: there are many evil deeds done in our sight, and such great harm taken that it seems to us impossible that things should ever end well. As we look at these, we sorrow and mourn for them, so that we cannot rest simply in the blissful beholding of God – as we should do. The cause is that when we use our reason only we are now so blind, so lowly and so simple that we cannot know the high marvellous wisdom, the power and the goodness of the blessed Trinity. This is his meaning when he said, 'You shall see for yourself that all manner of thing shall be well', as if he said: 'Accept things now faithfully and trustingly, and at the end you shall see fully in truth and joy.'

"So in those same six words, 'I may make all things well', I understand a mighty comfort in all the events that are still to come. There is a deed which the blissful Trinity shall do in the last day (if I see it aright); but what that deed shall be, and how it shall be done, is unknown to all creatures who are beneath Christ, and shall be so until the time when it shall be done. The goodness and love of God wants us to know that it *will* be done. But his wisdom, by that same love, prefers to hide and conceal from us what it will be, and how it shall be done. The reason why he wants us to know about it is because he wills us to be easier in our souls and peaceful in loving, putting aside all those troubles in the world which could hinder our true joy in him.

"This is the great deed ordained by our Lord from without-beginning, treasured and hid in his blessed breast, known only to himself, by which he shall make all things well. For just as the blessed Trinity made all things from nothing, right so that same blessed Trinity shall make all well that is not well.

"In this sight I marvelled greatly and saw our faith. I mean this: our trust is grounded in God's word; and it is part of our faith to believe that God's word shall stand on all points. One point of our faith is that many creatures shall be damned – for instance the angels who fell from heaven because of their pride . . . and man whose faith has died in the holy Church . . . and also man that has received christening but lives an unchristian life – all these shall be damned to hell without end, as Holy Church teaches me to believe. In view of all this it seemed to me impossible that all manner of things should be well according to how our Lord had showed me in this time. But I had no other answer given to this difficulty except this: 'What is impossible to you is not impossible to me; I shall keep my promise in all things – I shall make all things well.'

"Here was a teaching which said that I should steadfastly remain true to the faith as I had originally understood it, and yet at the same time I should take my stand on and sincerely believe what our Lord showed at this time – that 'all manner of things shall be well'. For this is the great deed that our Lord will do, in which he shall keep his word in all things – he shall make well all that is not well. But what the deed will be and how it shall be done, there is no creature that knows or shall know until it is done – such was the understanding that I had of our Lord's meaning at that time."

It is worth noting that to Julian sin was far more formidable than pain or unhappiness. As Thouless points out: "Probably this is a fundamental difference between the medieval point of view and our own. We have at the back of our minds a conviction that the universe was created for us to be happy in, and we find it difficult to reconcile the fact that we suffer with our belief in the goodness of God. The medieval mind had no such tender concern for human suffering. Medieval institutions had not happiness as their object, and they inflicted unnecessary suffering with a callousness which shows a totally different attitude towards the world from that of a modern humanitarianism. Devout thinkers, such as Julian, regarded the world as a creation for the purpose of promoting the glory of God, and human beings as instruments for doing his will. They were perplexed at the difficulty of reconciling human failure to do God's will with their belief in God's omnipotence. So the problem of pain (which is so real to us that churches can be filled when a preacher promises to say some new thing about it) meant little to them, while their problem of sin grows less and less oppressive to the typically modern mind."

Julian ends her chapters on sin by asking us to make the very difficult distinction between man and deed: "God wills that we should hate the sin in itself, and always love the soul of the sinner in the same way that God loves it . . . these words then that God spoke to me – 'I keep you most surely' – are an endless comfort."

And later she said, "In this he brought to my mind the proper quality of a glad giver. A glad giver ever takes but little heed of the thing he gives; all his desire and intent is to please and to comfort him to whom he gives it. And if the receiver takes the gift gladly and thankfully, then the courteous giver sets at naught all his cost and labour, in return for the joy and delight he has; for he has pleased and comforted him he loves.

"Contemplate wisely as well the greatness of this word *ever*. For in it was showed a high understanding of the love that Christ has for our salvation, and all the joys that will follow from his passion. One is, he rejoices that he has done the deed and shall no more suffer. Another is that he has therewith brought us out of the endless pain of ignorance. Another is that he has brought us up into heaven, and has made us to be his crown and his endless bliss."

Such reflections were interspersed with her showings. In her eighth revelation she saw the actual bodily changes as death took Christ. It is an amazingly vivid passage, told with her usual clinical objectivity.

"I saw his sweet face as it were dry and bloodless with pale dying, then more pale, deathly, languishing; then it changed to a bluish tinge, and then the flesh turned a brownish-blue, more deeply dead . . . this changing colour was pitiful to see. And as well the inner moisture clotted and dried, clogging his nostrils, and his sweet body was brown and then black – the fair, fresh, lifelike colour changing and turning into this dying dryness.

And there was a sharp dry wind, fearfully cold . . . and the blood-loss and pain within and blowing of the wind and cold from without met together in the sweet body of Christ. And these four – two within and two without – dried up the flesh as time went on. And though the pain was bitter and sharp it was full long-lasting in my sight, and painfully dried up all the living spirit of Christ's flesh. So I saw the sweet flesh dry, part by part, with marvellous pain. And as long as any feeling was left in Christ's flesh he suffered. . . . The sweet body was so discoloured, so dry, so shrunken, so deathly and so piteous, it seemed to me he had been seven nights in death, continually dying. And I thought the drying of Christ's flesh was his greatest pain, and the last, of his passion."

During this vision she remembered the words that Jesus spoke on the cross: 'I thirst'. She saw two meanings in this, one spiritual and the other physical. She saw that he longed to draw men up out of their ignorance and into his bliss; and also she saw – and this was more important to her at the time – his bodily pain of thirst as his moisture dried. She describes the agony of the tearing flesh as the weight of the body prised it loose from nails and thorns; and then she saw the body beginning to lose weight as it dried out.

She tells us how the pain of her sympathy for this agony almost made her repent of her wish to share in his death: "The showing of Christ's pains filled me with pain. For though I knew he suffered just the once, yet he wanted to show me his pain and fill my mind with it, as I had once asked of him. In all this time of Christ's presence I felt no pain except his pain. Then it seemed to me that I had known very little what his pain was when I asked for it; and like a wretch I was sorry for myself, thinking that had I known what it was like, I would have been loath to ask for it. For my pain seemed to pass beyond any death of the body, and I thought: 'Is there any pain in hell like this?' And I was answered in my mind: 'Hell is a different place, for there is despair.' Of all the pains that lead to salvation this is the most pain – to see your lover suffer. How could any pain be worse than to see him that is all my life, all my bliss, and all my joy, suffer? Here I felt steadfastly that there was no pain that could be suffered like that sorrow I had when I saw him in pain."

The pitiless realism of these descriptions that Julian gives may repel us, in our more squeamish age, so that we decide to dismiss her as a morbid hysteric. But to do so would be a mistake. Her visions contain an essential truth, one which is often evaded in conventional, bland religion. It is the truth of suffering, and of great suffering, which is the basic state of us all. 'I teach nothing but suffering and the way out of suffering' said the Buddha, knowing pain to be at the root of our lives.

And, as Thouless says, "It may be doubted whether our rejection of 'morbidity' is entirely a gain. Death, failure, and misery become no less real because we have lost our feeling of reality about them. We may 'healthy-mindedly' refuse to face the fact, but fact it remains, that the end of all our earthly struggles, hopes, and loves is death and bodily decay. We have attained 'healthy-mindedness' by thrusting these facts out of the region of conscious recognition. In the rare moments of realisation when they force themselves into consciousness they are an unresolved terror before which we quail until we can again attain confidence by the redirection of our energy towards the business of living."

In the main, then, rejection causes most of our suffering. We are always trying to have what we want rather than what we don't want, and this leads to a ceaseless and relentless effort to try to change situations rather than to live them through to their very end. But when we reject, move away, or alter things to suit ourselves, we do not always get rid of such situations. Our clinging to what we want rather than to what we have got may turn what we have got into an ignored but still undigested lump remaining inside us.

The robust realism of the Middle Ages did not flinch from or try to disguise what is unpleasant. Julian was with, and not shuddering away from, her image of Christ in his pain. The physical realities of life and death were part of religion, not divorced from it. In such an attitude there was courage and honesty and genuine depth of feeling.

In our lives today, how many of us actually feel very much? We seem to have devised so many escape routes from the painful and yet infinitely rewarding task of really living that we are on the way to becoming a planet of non-humans. Our restless search to fill mind and emotions with titillating distractions such as continuous radio and television, means we have turned life into a non-stop circus which we watch, like mindless animals, but take no part in.

Julian's life was lived in the opposite way. She wanted to identify with at least one thing, Christ's agony and death, to the very limits of her nature. It may seem a strange desire, but it was not strange in her culture. And in general religious practice it is not at all unusual, rather it is often regarded as one of the 'ways'. In Tibetan Buddhism, for instance, (whose goal is to be one with the Origin and to know Suchness as oneself), it is felt necessary to bring everything into the light of day so that it may be recognised – for if we are unaware how we function we will not use the energies of which we are composed for anything but the satisfaction of immediate desires. Consequently death and destruction of the body must be seen and accepted and to this end the practitioner is advised to sit in a graveyard where the bodies lie unburied (in Tibet bodies are compassionately offered for food for animals and birds) and there to meditate on the transitory nature of life and on the equality and sameness of all created things. Surrounded by rotting flesh, he should reflect that there is no intrinsic difference between an attractive object and a repellent one. All are manifestations of this world and it is only the mind which discriminates and produces feelings of desire or repulsion. To be undisturbed by *all* worldly sights leads to tranquil fearless-ness and there is no doubt that Julian, after really looking at the rotting flesh of Christ, acquired a depth of tranquillity and non-attachment which she might not have found in any other way. Her 'meditation' was to saturate her mind with the details of death so that she could be as fully conscious of it as possible. Then, as with the Tibetan graveyard method, she could develop an attitude to living which contained and included death but which took away its power to terrify.

Both Ruysbroeck and Eckhart tell us of the 'taste' of God. This is the reality which cannot be defined because it goes beyond any definition. We can see this in a very simple way. We can talk about a lemon in words – yellow, oval, cool, smooth – but in order to know what it is really like we have to drink the juice and taste the flesh. If you sip the sea but once, said Zen Master Dogen, you will know the taste of all the oceans in the world. The real tasting of life comes when we are no longer content with thoughts and ideas about it but want the direct unmediated experience of it. Julian wanted to go beyond all thoughts about Christ and to know him 'bodily' – the very taste of him. So she accepted all his pain and suffering and identified with it, knowing it to the full extent of her capacity.

"Thus I chose Jesus for my heaven, whom I saw at that time only in pain. I wanted no other heaven than Jesus, who shall be my bliss when I am there. And this has always been a comfort to me; that I chose Jesus for my heaven in all his time of agony and sorrow; and it has been a teaching to me that I should always do so and choose only him for my heaven, in well-being and in woe."

She describes how she was released from her pain: "Suddenly, while I was still beholding the cross, he changed to a blissful expression of face. The changing of his expression changed mine, and I was as glad and merry as it is possible to be. Then our Lord brought merrily into my mind: 'Where is there now any point to your pain or your grief?' And I was full merry . . . and then he said, 'My dear darling, I am glad you are come to me; in all your woe I have ever been with you. And now you see me in my love and we are oned in bliss.'

"He then asked her: 'Are you well paid that I suffered for you?' I said: 'Yes, good Lord, by your mercy; yes, good Lord, blessed may you be.' Then said Jesus, our good Lord: 'If you are paid, I am paid. It is a joy, a bliss and an endless liking to me that ever I suffered passion for thee. And if I could suffer more, I would suffer more.'"

We can see this exchange as the asking of a profound and illuminating question – 'Are you well paid?' Are you satisfied? Is the God-ground enough for you? This is the question that we all should, in deep honesty, ask ourselves. Is it enough? Is there enough meaning in our religious intuition to give us ultimate satisfaction? And if not, where will we find it? Julian had no doubt of her answer – '*Yes*, good Lord'.

In her straightforward way (which may appear childish to some of her readers but not to others) she continued to question God. She pondered on the thought that 'if sin had not been we should all have been clean and like to our Lord – as he made us'. She wondered why sin had not been prevented by the wisdom of God, for then, she thought, '*all* would have been well'.

She was answered by Jesus, who told her: "Sin must needs be." By this she understood him to mean all that is not good. Then he added, "But all things shall be well and all shall be well, and all manner of things shall be well." These words, she said, "were showed full tenderly, showing no blame towards me nor anyone".

Here we come to Julian's most personal revelation. Her vision of sin and of the love of God were realistic. She saw sin as it was, in all its suffering and tragedy – having as its symbol the agony on the cross – and not only that but she saw that evil will always be in the world – 'Sin must needs be' – and she even foresaw a time when "Holy Church shall be shaken with sorrow and anguish and tribulation in this world, as men shake a cloth in the wind". But to this God answered her: "'A great thing I shall make of this in heaven – a thing of endless worship and everlasting joy'; so much so that our Lord, as I saw, rejoices in the tribulations of his servants, but with pity and compassion. On every person that he loves, in order to bring them to his own bliss, he lays something, which, although it does not make them in any way offensive in his sight, is a reason why they are humbled and despised in this world, scorned and mocked and rejected. This he does to prevent them taking harm from false pride in themselves, from vanity and from too much glorying in worldly power – and to help them to find the way by which they will come to a bliss which is real and without end. For he says: 'I shall wholly break you of your vain affections and your destructive conceit; and after that I shall gather you and bring out humbleness in you, healthiness and holiness by oneing you to me.' And then I saw that all the kind compassion a man has for his even-Christians – this is Christ in him.

"The same act of being brought to naught that he showed in his passion – it was showed again here, in this compassion; for there are two ways of understanding this, according to our Lord's meaning. One is of the bliss which comes to us, wherein he wills that we have great joy; the other is, of the comfort in our pain – that we may know that it will all turn to our profit because of his passion; and that we may know that we suffer right nothing alone, but with him; that we may see him, our ground; and that we may see that his sins and his suffering so far surpass all that we might suffer, that it cannot be truly comprehended.

"Contemplating this will save us from unhappiness and despair in feeling our pain. And although we see truly that pain comes about through our own self-love and desire and is deserved by us, yet his love excuses us. Of his great courtesy he does away with all our blame, and looks at us with forgiving and pity, as children innocent and lovable."

Although records tell us that Julian was an educated woman, her contacts with the outside world through her window would be mostly with simple, uneducated people, who were likely to ask such basic questions as: "What is the use of praying when God does not answer?" or "Does he not already know what we want without any prayers?" However simple the enquiry, her replies would be usually on a deeper level, thus drawing the questioner away from his self-concern to a broader viewpoint. On one occasion, she tells us, she erred and was gently reproved. She had asked God about a certain person she loved, what was to happen to this person. "And in this desire to know, I obstructed myself, for I was not given knowledge at that time. But I was answered in my understanding, as if by a friendly man: 'Take it generally and behold the courtesy of your Lord God as he shows it to you. For it is more worship to God to see him in everything, than in any one special thing.' And if I should act wisely, in accordance with this teaching, I should not be glad for any special thing nor distressed by any manner of thing; for *all* shall be well."

Her way of teaching was undoubtedly that of saying aloud what she wrote in her books. For instance, she might have taught this prayer, one that she heard God say to her: "I it am. The greatness and goodness of the Father, I it am; the wisdom and kindness of the Mother, I it am; the light and grace that is all blessed love, I it am; I it am, the Trinity; I it am, the Oneness; I it am, the highest goodness of all things. I it am that makes you to love. I it am that makes you to long. I it am, the endless fulfilling of all true desires."

At other times she would probably advise from her own experience. In her fourteenth revelation she saw two conditions for prayer: "one is rightful [praying for the right thing], the other is sure trust. For often we do not fully trust; we are not sure that God hears us because (so we imagine) of our unworthiness and the fact that we feel nothing at all – for we are often as barren and dry after our prayers as we were before. So our imagination and our folly is the cause of this weakness of ours; and this by my own experience."

When she put this to her Lord, he answered her: "I am the ground of your beseeching. First, it is my will that you have it – and seeing that I made you to desire it, and seeing that I made you to beseech it and you do beseech it, how could it then be that you should not have your beseeching?" She then saw that God himself wills us to want God. "Our Lord", she said, "is full of mirth and gladness because of our prayer. For it makes us as like to him in our conscious mind as we are in our soul . . . he spoke to me thus:

" 'Pray inwardly, although there seems to be no savour in it, yet it is profitable. Pray inwardly, even though you think you cannot, for in dryness and barrenness, in sickness and in feebleness, then is your prayer full pleasant to me (even though you have little savour for it!). And so is all your real prayer in my sight.'

"Some of us believe that he is all-mighty and *may* do all," added Julian, "and that he is all-wisdom and *can* do all. But that he is all-love and *will* do all, *there* we fall short.

"God is nearer to us than our own soul. For he is the ground in whom our soul stands; and he is the means which keeps the substance and senses together, so that they shall never part. For our soul sits in God in very rest; and our soul stands in God in sure strength; and our soul is kindly rooted in God in endless love. And therefore, if we want to have knowing of our soul, and communion and loving with it, we need to seek into our God, in whom it is enclosed."

Julian undoubtedly had the feeling of no-self, of being deeply oned in transcendent union beyond all barriers, when she was in contemplation. She describes how the soul is led to a great desire to be oned with God, with that which is unconditioned: "And then shall we, by his sweet grace, in our own surrendering continuous prayer, come to him now in this life by many personal touchings of sweet spiritual sights and feelings, measured to us according to our own simplicity. And this is done by the Holy Ghost until we die in longing for love. And then shall we come to our Lord, ourselves clearly knowing him and God fully having us; and we shall endlessly be had by God; seeing and fully feeling him and spiritually hearing him and delectably inbreathing him, and of him we shall sweetly drink.

"And then we shall see God face to face, homely and fully. The creature that is made shall see and endlessly behold God which is the Maker. For no man may see God in this way and yet continue to live in this deadly life. But when God of his special grace shows himself here, he strengthens the creature above itself to receive the experience of him, and he measures the showing as is right for the occasion."

With such insights, Julian lived in the company of God. Such very personal spiritual company may not suit us all. Yet Julian never experienced that fatal limiting and domesticising of the God-ground which so often goes with strong personalisation of it. Rather, her Lord was infinitely flexible and accommodating, uniting homeliness and majesty, time and timelessness, body and spirit, in one reality.

"Nature has been tested in the fire of tribulation, and in it was found no lack of defect. Thus are nature and grace of one accord. For grace is God, and unmade nature is God also. He is two in manner of working but one in love; and neither of these works without the other – they cannot be parted."

In this way Julian combined the very great and the very small – but perhaps it was the small that her peasant friends loved most, and where Julian's joy in her Lord showed itself best.

"Full merrily", she wrote – and perhaps she also said it to one who was downcast and uncertain – "and gladly our Lord looked into his side and beheld it and said this word: 'Lo, how I loved you!', as if he had said: 'My child, if you are not able to look on my Godhead, see how I allowed my side to be opened and my heart cloven in two, so that all the blood and water poured out. And this gives me joy and so I want it to do to you.' This was what our Lord showed me to make us merry."

She saw Jesus as both father and mother – "for he would like to become fully our mother in all things" – and she described motherhood as being the kindest and readiest and most loving of states. Yet "we know that all our mothers bear us to pain and dying: a strange thing that!" she comments, "but our true Mother Jesus, he alone bears us to joy and endless living; blessed may he be!"

She saw us when we fall as needing the compassion of Mother Jesus:

"But often when our falling and wretchedness is shown to us we are so sore afraid and so greatly ashamed of ourselves that we scarcely know where to go. Yet even then our courteous Mother does not want us to flee away; nothing could be more displeasing to him. Rather, he wants us to be like a child. For when it is distressed and afraid it runs hastily to the mother. And if it can do nothing else, it cries to the mother for help with all its might. So will he have us behave as the meek child, who says: 'My kind Mother, my gracious Mother, my most dear Mother, have mercy on me. I have made myself foul and unlike you; and I cannot right it except with your help and grace.' And if we do not feel eased at once, then we may be sure that he is using the way of a wise mother. For if he sees that it is good to mourn and to weep for love's sake, he will suffer that with ruefulness and pity until the right time comes."

What comfort and reassurance her visitors must have had from Julian and how they must have loved her inner strength. What she received she gave and when God talked to her she gave his words to everyone, just as he had said them:

"See, I am God; see, I am in all things; see, I do all things; see, I never lift my hands off my work, nor ever shall; see, I lead each thing to the end that I make for it, from without-beginning and by the same strength, wisdom and love that I made it with. How should anything be amiss?"

In the stressing of the command *see*, Julian showed others how to contemplate by paying attention, by looking, and by trusting. There were surely many who felt their hearts full of trust when Julian said this to them, even more positively than before:

"Our good Lord answered all the questions and doubts that I might make, saying full and comfortably in this way: I will make all things well. I shall make all things well. I may make all things well, and I can make all things well; and so you shall see for yourself that all things shall be well."

Above all Julian *delighted* in Jesus. To be oned to him and to delight in him were her goals. And her delight took her to that miraculous land of awareness, to the new world within the known world, where the very air is alive with meaning and all things show a translucent innerness.

"Truth sees God and wisdom beholds God, and of these two comes forth the third, and that is a holy marvelling delight in God, which is love."

What was the meaning behind all her revelations? she queries, at the very end of her book. She was given an answer. "What, would you know your Lord's meaning in this thing? Know it well. Love was h:s meaning. Who showed it to you? Love. Why did he show it to you? For love. Hold to that within yourself. You shall know more of the same, but you shall never know other than love, without end."

"Thus", she says, "I learned that love is our Lord's meaning. And I saw full surely in this and in everything else, that before God made us, he loved us. And that love was never ended nor ever shall be. And in this love he has performed all his actions; he has made all things profitable to us. And in this love our life is everlasting. In our making we had our beginning: but the love wherein he made us is without-beginning. In which love we have our beginning. And all this shall we see in God without end."

St Bernard of Clairvaux

In Bernard we find a bridge between the two great ideals of mysticism – what might be called the way of emptiness and the way of fullness – which are described in the Introduction as darkness and light.

"Up noble soul! Out of yourself so far that you never come in and enter into God so deep that you never come out" said Eckhart, speaking for the empty, or dark, way. This is the way of non-attachment, of voidness of self, of the tasting of the God-ground beyond time and form; the way of losing the superficial self in the timeless 'isness' of Reality. Ruysbroeck, Eckhart and the author of the *Cloud* all extolled this way and found it the best. Not to *know about* but to *be* is the mark of this type of mysticism, and in surrendering all the hard separateness that belongs to our concepts of me and mine such a mystic pierces into the 'cloud of unknowing' and is oned with Reality in a way that is wordless and without manner.

"Song I call it," says Richard Rolle, "when in a fulfilled soul the sweetness of eternal love with burning is taken, and thought into song is turned, and the mind into full sweet sound is changed." Thus speaks the mystic of the way of fullness, or light; of the one who finds the God-ground not through detachment, as Eckhart advocated, but through loving devotion to all its expressions. In their different ways both Julian and Rolle found ease and freedom in adoring their creator as Person, and in filling themselves with the loving sweetness of the Personality.

Most mystics are predominantly one way or the other while sharing a bit of each, so to speak. But Bernard was finely balanced between the two and his powerful and enquiring mind was equalled by his passionate love of Reality, for he was able to outpour ecstasies of praise and love as well as, with intuition and common sense, to survey the path all men and women should follow. And everything that Bernard had to say about the spiritual path – and he wrote a great deal indeed – was also coloured by his own powerful character and the conflicts which he encountered both in himself and in his monks; indeed his well thought out and detailed sermons on the course of man's journey to his Origin greatly influenced the thinking of the later Middle Ages and, according to many, still influence Catholic theology today.

Yet for such a renowned teacher he is not quoted much or often referred to in the many anthologies and books on mysticism now in print. There are two possible reasons for this. His language, although he used it magnificently, yet remains somewhat earth-bound. He was perhaps more a preacher than a poet and the extraordinary mixture of the lyrical with the practical which comes from the pens of our three dark mystics was not his style at all. So in a sense what he says sounds unfashionable to our ears – his words are splendid and yet they do not contain the same intimate sublimity that we find in the *Cloud* and in Eckhart and Ruysbroeck.

The other reason is that Bernard was not at all influenced by the pseudo-Dionysius, whereas those three considered him to be their master. In so far as Dionysius' teaching appeals to us today – which it seems to very much – we are swung into tune with these three, whereas Bernard presents a more measured and formalised body of teaching.

Yet undoubtedly he reached their level of understanding – but seemed not to stay there. Often we find timelessness breaking through so that this patriarch, the last of the great Fathers, who lived so firmly in his century, seems suddenly free of himself. But on the whole his fascination lies more in his marvellous analysis of man and the way in which he faces us with our own condition. We are not easily enthralled by such a presentation (also practised in Zen), which may be another reason for Bernard's lack of modern popularity. Thomas Merton tells us that the whole purpose of the Rule of St Benedict (which Bernard followed) is, in Bernard's words, "to keep man in an atmosphere where, by obedience, poverty, solitude, prayer, fasting, silence, manual labour and the common life, he will be constantly running into occasions where he will be brought face to face with the truth about himself, and forced to recognise his misery without God, with the result that he will turn to God, begging for that grace which will enable him to purify his soul . . . and free the divine image within him".

There is little to get high on in such a path. And yet the constant reminder to drop our self-will is what the mystical journey is about, and Bernard is brilliantly able to set us on our course even if he does not come with us the full way.

Who was St Bernard? Seen from eight hundred years later, he appears a shining light in the darkness of the Middle Ages; a heroic, dedicated monk whose life transformed the times he lived in.

Bernard was born in 1090 at Fontaines les Dijon in France. His father was Tescelin, a Knight of Châtillon, and his mother Aleth, the daughter of Bernard of Montbard who was connected with many of the noble families of Burgundy. He was brought up in the Château of Fontaines les Dijon, which in the eleventh and twelfth centuries was nothing like it is today, being little more than a fortified stone keep. Bernard was the third son of seven children, six boys and a girl, and according to legend Aleth dreamed before his birth that she bore a barking dog in her womb. She was told by a hermit that this meant the child would be a great preacher and bark in defence of the Church!

Perhaps this story influenced his parents – or possibly the innately spiritual character of Bernard revealed itself very early. For while the other sons were kept at home, Bernard, at the age of six or seven, was sent to school with the Canons of St Verle at Châtillon, some fifty miles away. Tescelin had a house in Châtillon and Aleth spent much of her time there. Records tell us that she was a devout woman who had been about to enter a convent when the Lord of Fontaines asked for her hand in marriage. She accepted him but lived more as a nun than as a grand lady. She nursed and cared for all her children herself and whatever spare time she had she gave to helping the poor and to prayer and meditation. She had a strong influence on Bernard's character and he adored her to the end of her rather short life.

Bernard stayed in Châtillon until he had finished his education. He was noted there for being a brilliant scholar and also for composing ribald verse, although this was later denied by his disciples. He was very popular, although in his teens so shy and sensitive with strangers that he could barely open his mouth. He suffered badly from migraine and continued to do so all his life. As he grew into manhood he developed great good looks of a rather fragile, unearthly kind. He was tall, willowy and blond and had eyes which were 'dove-like' (we are not told the colour – perhaps dove-grey). He was high-spirited and very charming but already with a will of iron in respect of his own character training. It is said that he once threw himself into an icy pond to calm his passion after he had exchanged glances with a girl.

A time of psychological crisis developed for him in his late teens when he faced the choice of becoming a monk or staying in the world. As the son of a noble family and as a very promising scholar with a real gift for writing and a deep love of it, he could have made a great career in the world, or in the Church as a bishop or cardinal. For some months, it is said, he was in a desperate state of indecision and was racked too by his own natural physical desires which, as a monk, he would have to deny. For he fully realised the power of sexual love and some historians say that he deliberately threw himself into a life of dissipation in order to make his decision. He knew that he could do nothing by halves – he must either plunge into the world and lead a pleasurable and ambitious life, or give himself completely to God.

He made his choice and to his family and friends it seemed a very strange one. He would be a monk: this they had expected. But whereas they had thought he would go to the great Benedictine house of Cluny, where life was not too severe and where he would have ample time for writing, they were shocked to learn that instead he intended to enter the poor and insignificant monastery of Cîteaux, a house built in an unhealthy swamp and renowned for the rate at which its monks died from fever or malnutrition.

There was a great outcry. Why did he want to bury himself in such a dreary, unwholesome spot, where his life would be one of endless hard labour? Later he himself gave his reply: "I chose Cîteaux in preference to Cluny not because I was not aware that the life of Cluny was excellent and lawful but because 'I am a thing of flesh and blood, sold unto the slavery of sin'. I was conscious that my weak character needed a strong medicine."

But, to begin with, family opposition was too strong, and Bernard gave in and agreed to postpone his final decision until he had been to Germany to finish his literary studies. This was a clever ruse of his brothers because the one thing Bernard cherished as a personal ambition was to excel in writing. In fact it is said that he gave up everything when he became a monk except the art of writing superbly.

He was to leave Châtillon in the autumn, but before departing he rode off to say goodbye to his brothers. The road he followed wound through the beautiful countryside of Burgundy but as he went he began to feel a strange uneasiness. His mother had died a few years earlier, to his great sorrow, but suddenly he thought he saw her standing by the roadside and looking at him with sadness in her eyes. He jumped off his horse and went into a small chapel nearby and when he came out his heart was transformed. There was to be no literary career, no Germany, but instead he would go to Cîteaux at once – and rather than saying goodbye to his brothers he would take them with him!

Bernard never fully revealed the content of that experience in the chapel, but later on in his life he was to say: "Blessed and holy should I call one to whom it has been granted to experience such a thing in this mortal life at rare intervals, or even once, and this suddenly, and for the space of hardly a moment. For in a certain manner to lose yourself as though you were not, and to be utterly unconscious of yourself and to be emptied of yourself, and as it were brought to nothing, belongs to heavenly conversation, not to human affection."

Whatever he experienced, it changed his life totally. His divided mind was resolved and he was a whole man once more. Undoubtedly he felt that a surrender had been asked of him and he was only too glad to give it. No more dilly-dallying with literature and the subtleties of fine writing. This occupation, when compared to the true desire of his heart now revealed to him, faded into nothing. From then on he was single-minded in his dedication to the spiritual life.

A great energy and fervour rose up in him. He rode on to Grancy to look for his brothers, Guy and Gerard, but they were not there. They had set off to meet him and must have passed him by when he was in the chapel. So he went to his uncle, Gaudry, who, infected by his enthusiasm, agreed to enter the monastery with him. Then the brothers Andrew and Bartholomew were found and both capitulated. Guy and Gerard did not give in quite so easily. Guy was married and naturally felt he could not leave his family. But Bernard spoke to his wife and she went to Guy begging him with tears in her eyes to let her go to a convent – such were Bernard's powers of persuasion! So Guy was released from his marriage vows.

Gerard was inclined to dismiss all Bernard's plans as scatter-brained, and perhaps one can understand why. But Bernard would suffer no obstacles and he prophesied that Gerard would come too. "You are closing your heart to the grace of God," he told Gerard, "but it will find a way through a wound in your side." Two weeks later Gerard, a soldier, was wounded in his side and taken prisoner. "From now on I am a monk of Cîteaux!" he exclaimed, and was allowed to go free to join his brothers.

Even the youngest, Nivard, a child too young to be a monk, wanted to go with them. "See, Nivard," said Guy, the eldest, to him, "all our lands will now fall to you alone." To which the boy replied, "What – heaven is to fall to you, and earth to me? That division is not fairly made." He too went to Cîteaux soon.

Bernard's enthusiasm was at boiling point and it swept away not only his brothers and at least two uncles but also many of his friends. All over the countryside his eloquence and passionate conviction caused 'mothers to hide their sons from him and wives their husbands'. Nowadays, judging by the way society reacts to religious fervour, we would probably accuse Bernard of brain-washing and kidnap his converts back from him, but in the Middle Ages a young man was allowed to choose his own religious life even if it saddened those close to him.

Consequently in the spring of 1113 a band of at least thirty noblemen, probably more, presented themselves at the gates of Cîteaux.

"What do you seek?" asked Abbot Stephen Harding, according to ritual.

Bernard answered for them all.

"God's mercy and yours."

There is a web of cause and effect binding us together which sometimes seems to act in an uncannily appropriate way. It so happened that Bernard and his friends arrived just in time to prevent the closure of Cîteaux due to a lack of numbers. A strange history was attached to it, a history intimately related to the founding of the Cistercian Order, whose name in fact was taken from the mother-house, Cîteaux.

The great Order of St Benedict, which was founded in AD 529, had spread from northern Italy into the whole of western Europe and become a fine representation of the monastic ideal. The Benedictines were regarded with veneration and respect. But the Rule of St Benedict had not allowed for laxity and corruption within its own ranks. According to the Rule, each monastery was to be independent with no central overriding authority. Consequently when the first dedication and fervour had cooled down, some monasteries started to relax their practices and in the course of time this led to more and greater abuses until, as began to happen frequently, a reformation was found to be necessary. The reformers, zealous and ardent, usually founded new associations within the Order, hoping to restore and keep up the strict observance of the Rule. Among these reformers were the Cluniacs in 910, the Carthusians in 1084 and the Cistercians in 1100.

The Cistercians came into being when Robert, the Abbot of Molesmes in the diocese of Langres, an eager and uncompromising man, tried to tighten the lax rules of his community. Very few were prepared to back him although he insisted that many practices were falling short of the Rule. The whole issue was debated eagerly but the majority still refused to mend their ways. At the end of the struggle Robert left the monastery with six companions and journeyed to Cîteaux, a small estate given to them by the Duke of Burgundy, which was almost entirely undrained scrub, bog and forest. Soon afterwards they were joined by fourteen others and they set vigorously to work to build a house to shelter them and an oratory for their Offices, and to reclaim and cultivate the land.

Molesmes fell into worse disorder without Robert and he was peremptorily summoned back there by the Pope. His place at Cîteaux was taken by Alberic and when Alberic died by Stephen Harding who came from Sherborne in England. Stephen was a fine and good abbot but the daily regime was one of stark severity.

At two in the morning the great bell was rung and the monks immediately rose and hurried along the dark cloisters to the church. Then began Matins, which took about two hours. The next service, Lauds, came at dawn and during the interval (in winter a long one) the monk's time was his own to study or meditate. After Lauds he devoted himself to various religious exercises until nine when he went to work in the fields. At two he ate a meal. When it became dark he attended Vespers and at six or eight, according to the season, finished the day with Compline and then went to his dormitory.

This was a severe regime and one which the other Orders regarded with a feeling of stupefaction at the degree of inhuman asceticism shown. Later on it aroused a spirit of regeneration in the whole Church. But then it seemed an almost savage life of toil, and fewer and fewer aspirants came forward to take it on. The number also dwindled as deaths occurred and then, to make matters worse, an epidemic ravaged the countryside around and the monks, weakened by their abstemious way of life, died of it with terrifying rapidity.

"My heart is pierced with poignant grief", said Abbot Stephen, "when I think of that little band, the brethren; for we are dying daily, one after another, so that we are on the eve of seeing happen what I have so much feared, that our congregation will die out and disappear with us."

It was at this darkest point of its history that the Cistercian life was renewed by the arrival of Bernard and his friends at Cîteaux. With their coming the tide of bad fortune seemed to turn. News of the new life at Cîteaux spread like wildfire and encouraged others to come forward. Soon the small settlement was overflowing with enthusiastic young men and so great was the strength of the spiritual life set in motion by them that forty years later, at the time of Bernard's death, the Cistercian Order numbered over five hundred monasteries and people were saying that the whole world was becoming Cistercian.

Within two years of Bernard's arrival the numbers had grown to such an extent that Abbot Stephen decided to form four new monasteries. For the last of these he appointed Bernard as Abbot. The exact site had not been fixed; Bernard was left to choose this for himself, and in 1115 he set forth with twelve monks, among whom were three of his brothers.

About seventy miles north of Cîteaux they came to a valley where grew the famous plant, absinthe. The valley was open to the sun for the greater part of the day and had a clear stream winding through it. Bernard christened it Clairvaux, the Valley of Light, and he and his monks set to work at once to build their future monastery.

Shortly afterwards Bernard set off to secure confirmation of his appointment as Abbot. When William of Champeaux, the Bishop of Chalons-sur-Marne, and his clergy saw Bernard arriving with a companion, a sturdy middle-aged monk called Ebald, there was a good deal of speculation as to which was the Abbot, the robust Ebald or the frail young Bernard. But William knew at once and addressed himself straight away to Bernard. From that time onwards until his death six years later they were close friends and the monks of Clairvaux found a second home in Chalons.

Any friendly help was essential to them at this stage for the little settlement possessed no money or goods and precious little food. The land was not yet ready to yield a crop and the monks were living on what they could find – mostly wild carrots and berries. This was supplemented by a coarse bread. Bernard repudiated the idea that they should need anything more. The love of God and hard work should sweeten their daily bread and water, he told them.

It is true that when one lives in a simple and disciplined way the supposed need for variety and plenty seems a delusion of a sad nature. With no possessions a little to eat is a feast, every bite is appreciated and respected, and this can lead to a feeling of reverence for all that is manifested in the world. Yet there is a difference between living sparingly and actually starving and both Bernard and his monks were close to that latter condition.

Constantly they came to the end of their resources in that first year and constantly Bernard would exhort them to have faith. It always worked – unexpected gifts would arrive. But the cold of winter was dismal and their hunger undermined their faith. There is a story that when the majority had become quite desperate and begged to go back to Cîteaux, Bernard went off to pray. All the monks heard a voice say to him: "Rise, Bernard, your prayer is heard." While they were still discussing this a certain man arrived and gave them ten coins. A few minutes later another man came with a gift of thirteen coins, begging Bernard to pray for his son who was desperately ill. Bernard told him he would find his son recovered when he reached home, which he did, and from then on he constantly gave presents to the monastery.

Both Bernard and his monks found his unusual powers of prophecy and healing somewhat strange and embarrassing. His uncle Gaudry was highly sceptical and berated Bernard soundly for his presumption in thinking he could heal – until one day he himself was ill and begged Bernard to cure him. Bernard smiled and said he thought it would be too presumptuous for him to try, whereupon Gaudry pleaded that he had not really meant what he said about the miracles. Then, it is said, Bernard blessed him and cured him of both his illness and scepticism at the same time. Although many of the stories about Bernard have little factual basis, undoubtedly he did possess uncommon psychic gifts. We need not be as suspicious about these as Gaudry. The one thing we can be sure of is that the whole mystery of existence is never revealed, and although the psychic realm may not be evident or important to some of us, yet there are many who find it both compelling and helpful.

In one way and another the small community was saved. Bernard began to have more time to preach in the churches throughout the diocese and his personal magnetism began to draw great crowds. But the winter's austerity and his own love of ascetic extremes, as well as all the new activities, brought him to a very low state of health. He fell into such a state of collapse that the monks feared for his life. Just at that time Bishop William of Champeaux came to pay a visit. He was a calm man and he diagnosed that Bernard needed good food and plenty of rest. He arranged with the Chapter of the Cistercian Order that he should be put in charge of Bernard for a year – which meant he could exact complete obedience from Bernard. Bernard was relieved of all responsibilities. A small cottage was built for him just outside the monastery and a physician found to take charge of him.

This man is described by Bernard's biographers – and by Bernard himself – as both ignorant and tyrannical. Certainly he is said to have given Bernard some strange things to eat, such as blood in place of butter, and oil instead of water. The wretched Bernard found himself consuming three meals a day but gradually his strength came back. He accepted calmly the amount of food given to him and his reason for this was characteristic: that he enjoyed fasting and therefore he should eat!

One wonders at Bernard's delight in starvation. Had he discovered it as a way to unusual states of consciousness? Science has shown that when starved of nourishment the brain produces hallucinations and other strange states which might hold great attractions for a young religious seeker. Was Bernard's acceptance of food not only a means of getting well but also a corrective against the mind-blowing delights of starvation?

A year later he had recovered enough to begin his duties again as Abbot. But his digestion was impaired to the end of his life and he was always forced to keep a bowl beside him in which to vomit.

During the next eight or nine years he entered life fully, training his monks, preaching his sermons and establishing what came to be regarded as a Golden Age at Clairvaux. Men from all over Europe came to visit him. What was it that attracted them so much to the teachings of Bernard?

Essentially his teaching was about becoming free – a three-part freedom in which man finds himself, becomes himself, and knows himself to be one with God: "Let man seek his goods that are the most excellent in that part of himself which is above himself, that is, in the soul, where there is dignity, knowledge and virtue. By dignity in man I mean free will in which it is surely given him not only to excel, but to rule over all other living creatures; by knowledge, that by which he knows this dignity to be in himself, though not from himself; by virtue, that by which he then diligently seeks Him from whom he has his being, and cleaves firmly to Him when found."

What do we discover when we look at ourselves? Not only

the pleasures of the body but also the greatness of the spirit. Bernard chose the word *dignitas* to describe that essential ability to receive and respond, to act with responsibility and kindness, to be in harmony with the world as it is – all of which is the mark of the free man. But when a man calls himself free, what does it mean? To Bernard it meant those three things: to act wisely; to be aware that one's freedom to act is not created by oneself but comes from a transcendent Source; and then to search for that Source as for one's true identity.

To act without knowing that we are free is to behave like zombies. "Man made in honour, when he does not understand this honour, deserves by such ignorance to be likened to the cattle who are the sharers in his present corruption and mortality. Therefore it comes to pass that a man marked off by the gift of reason, through not knowing himself, begins to be herded with the flocks of irrational beings, while, ignorant of his own glory which is within, he conforms outwardly to things of the senses and is led away by his own curiosity; and he becomes one of the rest, because he does not understand that he has received something beyond the rest."

This is the world of suffering where a man identifies himself with all that is outside and sees himself only through the eyes of others. The world is then too real for him and through ignorance of his own free nature he ties himself to every object and gets carried away by every passing event.

He stands perpetually on the brink of twofold disaster. Either he does not comprehend his innate freedom and behaves as if he had none; or he is aware of it but does not realise or care about its origin. In the first instance he does not know his proper humanity, in the second he has fallen into self-centred conceit.

"Therefore we must greatly beware of this ignorance by which we think ourselves less than ourselves; but not less, but even more beware that by which we attribute more to ourselves; which happens if, deceiving ourselves, we think any good is in us and from ourselves. . . . This arrogance is seen to be even more dangerous than that first ignorance, for then God was not known, but by this he is condemned; it is worse and more detestable than the former, for by that we were made the fellows of cattle, by this the fellows of demons. Assuredly it is pride and the greatest of sins, to use gifts as though they were naturally ours, and to usurp the glory of the benefactor in the benefits we have received."

Man's initial error, then, is to fail to discover his own freedom. But this error is not so devastating as to know his freedom and accredit all its virtues to himself – indeed by doing this man denies to himself all the wonder and mystery of the Origin. This, to Bernard and to many mystical Catholics, is the real fall of humanity, the sin of glorifying ourselves for that which we did not create and which is not ours to own. Perhaps Bernard would have agreed with the *Bhagavadgita*: "The activity of the world is a prison until actions are performed as worship of God. Therefore you must perform every action sacramentally and be free from all attachment to results."

It was an essential part of Bernard's teaching (and he often stated that he brought forth nothing which had not been taught before) that man's greatest obligation is to turn to God and to discover his own reality – the third part of the free-will action. To Bernard it was a conscious and marvellous duty, but we might also see it as an urge which is at the root of many of our own actions. Jung once said that almost all the problems brought to him were basically religious ones, and it is likely that from our earliest moments we are in quest of that truest of all delights and fulfilments which comes only when the feeling of 'me' has been dropped.

How, then, did Bernard see such a discovery being made? Basically through selflessness and love.

"For God, who, in his simple substance, is all everywhere equally, nevertheless, in his working, is in rational creatures in a different way than he is in others and in the good ones in a different way than he is in the bad. He is in irrational creatures in such a way as not to be comprehended by them; by all rational ones, however, he can be comprehended through knowledge – but only by the good is he comprehended also through love. Only in the good, therefore, he is – and in such a way as to be also with them by harmony of will; for as they subdue their own wills to rightness so that it is not unworthy of God to will what they will, they are particularly joined to God by not dissenting from his will."

Thus to direct his own will to loving God (that which we can also term the essence and reality of our lives) with a totality and unreservedness which he could never give to any created thing, was to Bernard the essential practice of his life. Here we see the mirror of ourselves. If we can but turn away from the world of things, even just briefly, we come across an inner stillness and depth in which a new world within the known world arises. Meaning and significance in all things becomes apparent against our frequent grey background of frustration, boredom and despair. To make the effort – perhaps this is what is really meant by worship – "This alone is true realisation, wherein one knows oneself in relation to that Reality, attains peace and realises one's identity with It" (Ramana Maharshi).

It might have interested Bernard to know that, according to the latest discoveries of quantum physics, even at the subatomic level there is choice – some might even call it freedom of will – because atomic phenomena can only be described in probability patterns, never with certainty. This led the physicist, H. P. Stapp, to formulate the belief that: "An elementary particle is not an independently existing un- analysable entity. It is, in essence, a set of relationships that reach outwards to other things."

In an experiment involving pairs of photons (particles of light), the passage of one photon was deflected by a polariser in such a way that it was impossible for the other to know what its partner was doing. The measurement clicks for each showed, however, that the particle in area B somehow knew, at the moment that it happened, that the state of its space-separated partner in area A had changed, and as a result *it changed its own state accordingly* – at least, that is the conclusion drawn by the physicist, David Bohm.

Such can almost be described as an act of conscious free will and indeed the physicist, E. H. Walker, believes that consciousness explains our universe: "Consciousness may be associated with all quantum mechanical processes . . . since everything that occurs is ultimately the result of one or more quantum mechanical events, the universe is 'inhabited' by an almost unlimited number of rather discrete, conscious, usually nonthinking entities that are responsible for the detailed working of the universe."

Bernard (like the Buddha in his time) was concerned that

people should become fully conscious and that they should be helped to see that the effort of free will, of self-transcendence, was not only imperative but also psychologically practical. In this way they should grow in gradual stages to full realisation.

First, said Bernard, they must become aware of their own condition – that they are of necessity bound by the body and that the first love they will experience will be centred on themselves. This love he called 'carnal', or bodily, and his own definition was: "carnal love is that love by which man loves himself for his own sake and before all else". Carnal love is indeed what we are born with and at least in the early years our own needs always take priority. Small children are wholly absorbed in their own affairs and this simple egotism has its own innocence and place and contains no element of depravity.

So to Bernard the natural state of man, although ignorant, is not in itself unhealthy, and as long as man stays within the simple demands of his life his mind too will be pure. But when he begins to demand pleasures for their own sakes, pleasures that are far removed from necessity, his purity becomes corrupted.

At this point in Bernard's teaching we approach the sticky waters of the Christian view of the Fall of man – sticky because Christian dogma is itself not clear on what it means. Basically it seems that Christianity presupposes a state of perfection in which man, although separate from the God-ground, was still one with it in heart and mind and was transparently sinless in his actions, and unselfconscious. But after the Fall and the change from transparency to cloudy self-dominated motives, there was no longer such a perfect state, and the very Fall itself was occasioned by man's putting the love of self before the love of God. So he retained the image of God – the very innermost part of ourselves – which is ingrained in him, but lost the outer likeness to God.

There is a Fall in most religions. In Buddhism it is compared to a dance in which the dancer begins to become conscious of himself as separate from the dance; and then the person, the music and the dancing all separate out and that leads eventually to the dancer's conviction that he is the controller of the dance.

The story of the Fall was very important to Bernard. Because of it he believed that to love the God-ground and to be at one with it is fundamentally natural to man, for that is how he is made – and when he denies this innermost image he deforms his whole nature. "The soul begs its bread of another because it has forgotten how to eat its own; it runs after the things of the earth simply for lack of meditating the things of heaven." The Fall, then, was caused as Bernard saw it by craving for self-existence, which is how other religions see it too.

He continues: "The fact that Scripture speaks of our present *unlikeness* to God does not mean the likeness has been destroyed, but that something different has been drawn over it, concealing it. Obviously the soul has not cast off her original form but has put on a new one foreign to her. The latter has been added but the former is not lost, and although that which has been placed on top has managed to obscure the natural form, it has not been able to destroy it. St Paul laments that the gold has lost its brightness and that the finest colour has been obscured; but the gold is still gold, and the original base of the colour has not been wiped out. And so the simplicity of the soul remains truly whole in its essence, but that wholeness is no longer able to be seen now that it is covered over by man's deceit, pretensions and hypocrisy."

How to put things right? There have always been two ways of dealing with man's wrongly directed desires, particularly those that seek to put himself in place of the God-ground and to make his own ego the centre of the universe. One way is to destroy those desires or extinguish them by great efforts of self-control so that eventually a man comes to have strong discipline over himself, often believing that this will gain him a higher place in a future world or future life. The danger of this way is that it leads to power and the ego risks becoming inflated. The other way is to transform the desires themselves so that all man's fires become transmuted into their own heights. This is the way of powerlessness because it is calling upon the God-ground, upon man's innate sense of truth and reality, to come to his aid and redeem that which is false. One could describe the two ways as trusting only in oneself or trusting in that which is beyond oneself (in the sense that it is innately a part of oneself but not a part one is in touch with). Bernard preferred the latter.

"As a drop of water mingled in wine is seen to pass away

utterly from itself, while it takes on the taste and colour of the wine; as a kindled and glowing iron becomes most like the fire, having put off its former and natural form; and as the air, when flooded with the light of the sun, is transformed into the same clarity of light, so that it seems to be not merely illumined but the light itself – so it will needs be that all human affection . . . will then, in some ineffable way, melt from itself and be entirely poured over into the will of God.''

"Who is God?" he asked – and by this sort of question affected the thinking of future mystics such as Eckhart and the author of the *Cloud* – "I can think of no better answer than He who is. Nothing is more appropriate to the eternity which God is. If you call God good, or blessed, or wise, or anything else of this sort, it is included in these words, namely, He is."

Bernard believed that the very restlessness man always exhibits is due to the fact that he is unconsciously searching for that which is better than he can ever find in the world – his 'isness'. His search is inevitable and so too is the inevitability of the wreckage he leaves strewn behind him, because the sort of love he longs to give is not suitable for any finite object. Yet directed in the right way this very restless energy can help him to discover the fulfilment he longs for.

"Freedom", says Harry Williams, "does not consist in the ability to choose what is wrong but in the ability to be what we are."

Man is an exile, said Bernard, because he no longer inhabits the country of his birth. He has exiled himself from where he is like God to where he is unlike him and so has exchanged heaven for hell. But it is possible to reverse this process by the right use of free will. Unlikeness has not obliterated the basic image of God which forms us all (just as illness does not nullify the genes which characterise us). The reflection of God within us can be hidden but it cannot be destroyed. But the *likeness* to God – that can be both hidden and lost when the will is turned towards the world and when we no longer love properly but become subject to fear for ourselves instead. 'Perfect love casteth out fear' and it can surely be said that perfect fear casteth out love. Yet in spite of the malformations of fear and hate, greed and delusion, the God-image imprinted on us cannot be effaced and so we still unconsciously long for the

God-ground. And love is still able to conquer fear and hatred and we still have the freedom to choose between them – if we exercise our free will to be true to our own innate God-pattern.

"For me to be a saint means to be myself. Therefore the problem of sanctity and salvation is in fact the problem of finding out who I am and of discovering my true self," said Thomas Merton, a modern Cistercian. He continues:

"Trees and animals have no problem. God makes them what they are without consulting them, and they are perfectly satisfied.

"With us it is different. God leaves us free to be whatever we like. We can be ourselves or not, as we please. We are at liberty to be real, or to be unreal. We may be true or false, the choice is ours. We may wear now one mask and now another and never, if we so desire, appear with our own true face. But we cannot make these choices with impunity. Causes have effects, and if we lie to ourselves and to others, then we cannot expect to find truth and reality whenever we happen to want them. If we have chosen the way of falsity we must not be surprised that truth eludes us when we finally come to need it."

"That which is truly yours is timeless and emerges from timelessness", says Bernard. "Why do you add to your soul an alien shape, a deformity which is strange to it? For that alien form which you have allowed to possess you, you now fear to lose; and that fear is a kind of colour which stains the free will and hides it beneath itself and renders it like itself. How much more worthy of your origin would it be that you should desire nothing so that you should fear nothing; and that thus guarding your inborn freedom from servile fear, your soul should remain in its pristine beauty and strength."

How, then, do we find our inborn freedom?

First, said Bernard, by recognising it. In this Bernard, like the Buddha before him, saw desire for self-powered existence as the prime cause of suffering.

"There is in the heart a twofold leprosy; our own will and our own judgement. Our own will I call that which is not common to us and to God and other men but is ours alone. That is, when we carry out our will, not for the honour of God, nor for the benefit of our neighbour but simply for ourselves alone. Self-will means to will things that are intended not to give pleasure to God or to be of any use to our brothers, but only to satisfy the selfish promptings of our own minds. Diametrically opposed to this evil is charity; and charity is God.

"Self-will, then, is ever in a state of implacable hostility to God and constantly wages the most cruel warfare against him. What is there that God hates or punishes more except self-will?

"If self-will were to cease to exist, there would be no more hell. For what fuel would there be to feed those flames if there were no more self-will? Even now in this life, when we feel cold or hunger or other such things, what is it that feels the suffering if not self-will? For if we willingly bear with these trials, our own will becomes the *common will*. What may be called our own will is really a kind of sickness and corruption of the true will; and it is this corrupt element that will continue to be the subject of every kind of suffering until it is totally consumed."

Go into your suffering and be at one with it, thus advises Bernard. Do not try to escape it or avoid it, for that is the self-willed attitude of rejection. When you feel cold or hunger, *really feel it*. Surrender yourself to it and know it for itself.

Our fears usually prevent us from experiencing life fully. We conceptualise future events and build up fear before the act takes place, thus adding another problem to the original one. People to whom danger has come suddenly, often say that they had no time to feel afraid. We fear most strongly when we conceptualise fear. But Bernard tells us that this mental build-up is brought about by the self-will which rejects unpleasant experiences, and that if we willingly accept what happens to us our self-will can change and become more true to ourselves – it then becomes the common will. The common will, to Bernard, meant being at one with one's true and common state as it was meant to be.

The philosopher Gurdjieff described this common state as the 'essence': "When we speak of inner development and inner change we speak of the growth of essence. The question now is not to acquire anything new but to recover and reconstruct what has been lost. . . ." Essence is the real individuality, he said, which is almost entirely dormant in most men.

And if we look at it through Taoist eyes, we can see that when we surrender to the Way we put ourselves in tune with existence and then what happens to us is not the problem it was. We feel cold or hunger – or sadness or frustration – but they do not topple us over because we are at one with them. We have accepted and not rejected our condition, and when there is no more fear there is no more struggle or panic. To accept a situation fully, however awesome it may seem to us in concept form, is to take the major part of the suffering out of it.

In Bernard's eyes, acceptance is our natural state and self-willed rejection is a perversion of that state. For him the will was undoubtedly our greatest faculty and the very highest state of the will was its union to the God-ground. Such union comes about, he said, when we have recovered our common will, when we are naturally unselfish and naturally loving with a spontaneous freedom which is in fact our inborn nature. So, as Merton remarks, the core of Cistercian mysticism came to be the re-establishment of the integrity of human nature – and to Bernard this meant a willing submission to the Benedictine Rule.

Becoming aware of the freedom to choose was the keynote of Bernard's teaching and it became the whole foundation of the Cistercian practice. To *know* – in the greatest and most sublime sense of the word – who and what we are, is to find freedom in our true identity and to live as fulfilled human beings.

"We become contemplatives", said Thomas Merton, "when God discovers himself in us.

"In order to know and love God as he is, we must have God dwelling in us in a new way, not only in his creative power but in his mercy, not only in his greatness but in his littleness, by which he empties himself and comes down to us to be empty in our emptiness, and so fills us in his fullness.

"My discovery of my identity begins and is perfected in these missions, because it is in them that God himself, bearing in himself the secret of who I am, begins to live in me not only as my Creator but as my other and true self.

"People", he adds, "who know nothing of God, and whose lives are centred on themselves, imagine that they can only find themselves by asserting their own desires and ambitions and appetites in a struggle with the rest of the world. They try to become real by imposing themselves on other people, by appropriating for themselves some share of the limited supply of created goods and thus emphasising the difference between themselves and other men who have less than them or nothing at all.

"They can only conceive one way of becoming real: cutting themselves off from other people and building a barrier of contrast and distinction between themselves and other men. They do not know that reality is to be sought not in divisions but in unity, for we are 'members of one another'."

Bernard would have wholeheartedly agreed with Merton, and in analysing man's condition as the basis of his teaching, Bernard brought himself within the comprehension of all men everywhere. No wonder he was popular. He always spoke straight to man's heart and often in words that few would dare to use today.

"Is it not shameful to lift up your head, you who dare not lift up your heart – to stand erect in body whose desire crawls upon the earth?. . . . Nevertheless since you were created to the image and likeness of God, your life, now become like to the beasts in losing its likeness, is still the life of God's image. If, therefore, even when you were clothed in your greatness you did not understand that you were slime of the earth, at least now take great care, now you are sunk into the slime of the abyss, not to forget that you are the image of God, and blush to have it covered over with an alien likeness. Remember your nobility and take shame of such a defection. Forget not your beauty, to be the more repelled at your hideous aspect."

'Remember your nobility . . . forget not your beauty . . .' – it was for love of God and delight in goodness that men were to change their ways. Compassion was to replace fear – compassion arrived at through great humbleness. Humility became Bernard's theme and he wrote about it constantly, not only as a way of opening oneself to the clarity of the God-ground but also as a means of practising open-heartedness to the world. This, for Bernard, took the form of charity to the poor. And being Bernard, ardent and fiery, he not only gave everything he had but insisted that others should do likewise. He wrote violent letters to the Cluniac abbeys, accusing them of self-indulgent luxury. His objection to their architecture, rich sculptures and ceremonial dress was for intellectual as well as moral reasons: "So great and marvellous a variety of diverse forms meets the eye that one is tempted to read in the marbles rather than in the books, to pass the whole day looking at these carvings one after another rather than in meditating on the law of God."

Here we meet the puritan Bernard, not altogether right in his assumptions perhaps (but he was a young man at the time). For there is no doubt that the senses are also our gateways, as well as the intellect, to the God-ground. Visual beauty can draw us close to the Mystery, as can the enchantment of music.

It is fair to say that Bernard had little visual sensitivity – he lived very much in his mind. A story is told that some people protested to him that he travelled the country preaching poverty but rode himself a very fine horse, richly caparisoned with gold and brocade. He was absolutely astonished and said that he had never noticed – he had never looked at the horse! From then on he rode a plain one.

Plain too were his churches, simple in design and bare of ornamentation: "The walls of the Church are indeed resplendent but her poor go in need", he roared at the abbots of Cluny. "She clothes her stones with gold and leaves her children to run naked. The eyes of the rich are flattered at the expense of the poor. The delicate find the wherewithal to gratify their taste, but the miserable find nothing to satisfy their hunger."

Behind all this invective was the noble idea that all men are born equal in their needs and that if all lived solely according to those needs there would be plenty for everyone. He was able to thunder. His own life was bare to the point of starkness. When there was starvation about he fed the local people. He inspired his monks to strip themselves that they might truly love their neighbour as themselves.

So to Bernard loving meant giving, and supreme love meant the gift of everything unconditionally. In this act was to be discovered a new state of being which he termed a fusion of the soul with God. This state was beyond all ideas or imagination and he would not tolerate such things as mystical dreams or supernatural visions. It was a state of pure likeness and in this likeness Bernard saw the whole of the pilgrim's spiritual path. For the more like God man becomes, the closer he grows to being one with the God-ground, with the intrinsic nature of existence itself. So to love oneself, once one realises who one truly is, is to unite with the Reality that is oneself. To know oneself is to know oneself as God, as Mystery, the God-ground, the Unconditioned, the Absolute. Thus eventually the creature is not abolished but transformed, consummated and realised.

"Love seeks no cause beyond itself and no fruit," said Bernard. "It is its own fruit, its own enjoyment. I love because I love; I love in order that I may love . . . of all the emotions and affections of the soul, love is the only one by means of which the creature, though not on equal terms, is able to treat with the Creator and to give back something resembling what has been given to it. . . . When God loves, he only desires to be loved, knowing that love will render all those who love him happy."

"You are good, O Lord, to the soul that seeks you: then what to her that finds? But here is a wonderful thing: no one can seek you save he who has first found. Therefore you will to be found that you may be sought, to be sought that you may be found."

"Let him kiss me with the kiss of his mouth", he says, quoting the Song of Songs. (Some of his best and most sublime writing is contained in his sermons on the Song of Songs.) The kiss of God's mouth is to Bernard what the 'taste of God' is to Eckhart. It is the experience which transcends all descriptions. In this he shows himself to be a true mystic in that he wanted no abstraction but the thing itself. He wanted to know the love of God not vaguely but passionately and specifically. "In this kiss there is no room for uncertainty or lukewarmness", he said; for to receive from God the 'kiss of his mouth' meant nothing less than the 'inpouring of the holy spirit'.

"It seems to me that He who said 'No man knoweth the Son but the Father; neither knoweth any man the Father but the Son, *and he to whomsoever the Son will reveal Him*' (Matthew 40:27) has here designated a certain kiss ineffable and unknown to any created being." In other words, we ourselves cannot create that extraordinary moment of new consciousness.

When it occurs it is at once recognisable as a new and unique experience – nothing has ever happened before which is in any way like it because it is out of time. So we can recognise it when it comes and even try to prepare ourselves for it; but it comes by gift only and is not an automatic return for our virtue. We cannot compel such a state to come to us but can only surrender ourselves to its mystery, as the bride surrenders in the Song of Songs. Such a surrender signifies great trust and love on our part and it is through this and not through techniques or virtuous behaviour that we find ourselves void of ourselves and at one with the Mystery itself.

But Bernard is emphatic that our trust and love must be genuine, which means that they are not based on blind credulity but on our intelligence, as well as our heart. And this intelligence should not be a mere wish for more knowledge but a deep longing for true wisdom.

"The teaching of the Spirit does not sharpen curiosity, but kindles compassion. Thus the Bride, when seeking him whom her soul loves, does not trust herself to superficial judgements nor does she follow the futile reasonings of human curiosity, but prays for this gift – that is, she entreats the Holy Spirit, so that through him she may receive at once the love for true knowledge and the seasoning of grace to accompany it. It is well said that this knowledge is accompanied by love, since a kiss is the sign of love. But the knowledge which puffs up is not given, as it is without love . . . and as a bee bears both honey and wax, so He has in himself both that which ignites the light of knowledge and that which infuses the taste of grace. Let not him who understands the truth but has no compassion, nor him who is all loving but does not understand the truth, think that he has received that gift, for in it there is no place for error or for lukewarmness. That is the reason why the Bride, in order to receive this twofold grace, presents her two lips; I mean the reason full of intelligence and the will full of love of heavenly wisdom."

In his insistence on both intelligence and love as necessary to enlightenment, Bernard shows himself to be thoroughly aware of man's greatest fulfilments, in much the same way as the Buddha.

Intelligence is a term, like love, which is often misunderstood. When it is turned outwards and used only for worldly benefit – and most people think of it solely in that way – it creates both pleasure and pain (of achievement and frustrated ambition) as do all our faculties when they are concerned only with the world. But when intelligence is turned inwards in a great surge of longing to discover the mystery of existence, it is our greatest ally and leads us to real wisdom – away from anger, delusion, attachment and strife, our worst enemies, and towards an abiding of the mind in clarity and calmness and selfless love.

"For there are two kinds of ecstasy in contemplation; one of the understanding, the other of the heart; one in the light of the understanding, the other in the movement of the heart; the one a blaze of discernment, the other a rapture of love" said Bernard.

The great strength of the Buddha's teaching was that he introduced his hearers to attitudes of mind rather than to doctrinal concepts. Thus the Dalai Lama could freely say (Westminster, July 1981) that he thinks of his religion less as Buddhism than as a religion of kindness – the label is less important than the attitude of mind. In the same way Bernard was very conscious that ultimate reality is linked to certain attitudes of mind and that our minds have to learn these attitudes, often with great difficulty. The monastic life was to him the perfect – indeed the only – way to set about this task. Hence his great fervour in creating monasteries and converting men and women to the religious life.

Not so many of us would agree with him nowadays. A Sufi, for instance, believes that the proper living of an ordinary life can contain some of the highest insights necessary, and that you can carry on a trade or occupation and yet (in secret, for Sufis never publicise their state of consciousness) live a life of real understanding. In Zen too the boatman who rows you across the river may well be a master, as may the local fisherman. But it is one of the limitations of Bernard's character – one in which he is time-bound in his own century – that for him only the monk or nun had a real chance of enlightenment.

Yet he was certainly right when he pointed out that we must find our own inner strength before we can teach others. It is through the act of contemplation (or meditation) that we come to this inner unity and only a monk, he thought, could be a real contemplative. Contemplation, for Bernard, was the highest form of the monastic life – and yet he was always aware that for many people action seems the better path. In many of his sermons he examined both the active and contemplative paths and came to the conclusion – one which is immemorial in mystical religion – that action based on contemplation is the best path of all. For action without contemplation is fraught with danger. When it springs spontaneously from a pure heart it cannot go wrong; but when over-involvement is present there is every likelihood that the action will not have good results.

"It appears to me that God's operation in us is twofold. There is one operation by which he establishes us in ourselves for our own enlightenment; and the other by which he adorns us outwardly with his gifts for our own profit and for the good of others. The first grace we receive for ourselves, the second for our neighbours. For example, faith, hope and charity are given us for ourselves; for without these we cannot be saved. But words of knowledge or of wisdom, the gift of healing, of prophecy and other powers – these are certainly bestowed on us only that they may be used for the benefit of our fellow creatures.

"But here we must take heed of two dangers; that of giving to others what is meant for ourselves and of keeping to ourselves what is given us for others. You are certainly retaining for yourself that which belongs to your neighbour, for instance, if you are given the gifts of knowledge or of eloquence – but fear, perhaps, or self-consciousness, or sloth, or an ill-judged humility restrains your good gift of speech in a useless, or rather, blameable silence. On the other hand, you dissipate and lose that which is your own if, before you have received a complete inpouring from God, while you are, so to speak, but half-filled, you rush to pour yourself forth. . . . You defraud yourself both of life and enlightenment when, without any right intention but puffed up by a wind of vanity, or infected by the poison of commercial reward, you thus impart everything to another; indeed what you thus communicate is merely the vomit which is swelling within yourself.

"If you are wise you will show yourself as a reservoir rather than as a canal. For a canal spreads abroad water as it receives it, but a reservoir waits until it is full before overflowing and so gives, without loss to itself, its superabundant water. But in the Church at the present we have many canals and few reservoirs. Many are those who pour all forth before they are themselves filled with it; they are more prepared to speak than to hear, are quick to teach that which they have not learned, and long to preside over others while they do not yet know how to govern themselves."

To guard against impetuous monks who thought themselves enlightened and wanted to change the world, Bernard pointed out that real action is a direct call from God. For those who did not have such a vocation it was better to live in 'contemplative idleness'. Ruysbroeck was later to use the same term 'idle' to convey the tranquil and sublime rest of the person, desireless and will-less, in his inner nature – a rest which is often the necessary forerunner of the truly active life. Such tranquil passivity, or perfect rest, easily brings about supreme activity. It is the healing work of the Ground – a healing and restoring to our original nature which cannot be accomplished when we are fruitlessly rushing about.

"Wisdom, when it enters, makes the fleshly sense taste flat, cleanses the understanding, heals and restores the palate of the heart. Once the palate is cleansed, it tastes what is good, it tastes wisdom, than which there is nothing better."

Never one to mince words, Bernard regarded as positively slothful the man or woman who preferred a feverishly active life to a harmonisation of activity with contemplation. Not only were they slothful but their easily distracted states of mind made them seem a mere rational sort of animal, not even up to manhood. One of the most important of his teachings is that Martha and Mary are sisters, living in the same house, and not enemies living apart. Both depend on each other and indeed complete each other, so that in our own natures we should always seek to harmonise the relationship between doing and being.

Buddhism, with its teaching of skilful means, says much the same thing. *Upaya* (skilful means) is the application of awareness or mindfulness to a situation to see in what way we can serve it best. Upaya demands flexibility and openness and an ability to observe without involvement. As an example, a gardener who is said to have 'green fingers', so that everything he plants grows well for him, is practising upaya in his garden, really seeing what is needed and supplying it at the right time and not supplying what is not needed. In the same way Bernard cautions against the false activity and temptation to pour out our ideas on others when we ourselves have not fully matured them, but instead to use the discretion of wisdom allied to a sincere faith, so that all that one does has both Martha and Mary as 'chamber companions'.

It took Bernard a good deal of time for such doctrines to be matured in his own mind. He had to learn a great deal by experience before he could expound them. The young Bernard, the newly appointed abbot whom we talked of earlier, needed to find wisdom to replace some of his reforming, puritanical zeal. Undoubtedly, with his great and ardent love for likeness to God, he drove his monks too hard at the beginning. Yet when tolerance and gentleness grew in Bernard they developed in a tender and motherly fashion, so that he could write to the parents of a young monk at Clairvaux: "Do not worry about the frail health of your son, for I shall look after him like a father and he shall be for me a son. I will be to him both a father and a mother, both a brother and a sister, and I will so temper and arrange all things for him that his soul may profit without his body suffering." This from the man who once would flee from visitors, putting tow in his ears so that he would not be distracted by idle conversation!

Nevertheless the realist in him kept his pen sharpened all his life. His correspondence became immense – over four hundred letters are now published and there must have been many more that are lost. A letter from Bernard was likely to be sharp and salutary, even to the Pope! St Hildegarde, a saint who received a number of rather astonishing revelations, once wrote to tell him that she had seen him in a vision as 'a man in the sun'. Bernard wrote back: "That other people should believe me better than I know myself to be, is an indication more of human stupidity than of any virtue in myself. . . ."

Bernard rarely spoke of himself or of his own inner experiences and at the beginning of his religious life appears not to have believed that mystical experiences really happened. But as his nature deepened he apprehended more and more of a new consciousness and towards the end of his life, in the 74th sermon of the Song of Songs, he described his own experience in this way:

"But now bear with my foolishness a little. I wish to tell you, as I have promised, how such events have taken place in me. It is indeed a matter of no importance. But I put myself forward only that I may be of service to you, and if you derive any benefit I am consoled for my conceit; if not, I shall have displayed my foolishness.

"I confess then that the Word has visited me, and even very often. But although it has frequently entered my soul, I have never at any time known the precise moment of its coming. I have felt that it was present. I remember that it has been with me; I have sometimes been able even to have a presentiment that it would come; but never to feel its coming, nor its departure. For whence it came into my soul, or where it went on quitting it, by what means it has made entrance or departure, I confess that I do not know even now. . . . It is not by the eyes that it enters, for it is without form or colour; nor by the ears, for it is without sound; nor by the nostrils, for it is not with the air but with the mind that it is blended . . . nor, again, does it enter by the mouth for it cannot be eaten or drunk; nor, lastly, is it capable of being traced by the touch, for it is intangible. By what way, then, has it entered? Or perhaps it did not enter at all, nor indeed come at all from outside. For it does not belong to any of those things which are external. Yet it has not come from within me, for it is good, and I know there is nothing good in me. I have ascended to that which is highest in me and lo! I have found the Word above me still. My curiosity has also led me to descend below myself and yet I have found it even deeper yet. If I have looked outside of myself, I have found it is beyond everything which is outside of me; and if within, it was at an inner depth still. And so I have learned the truth of the words which I have read: 'in Him we live and move and have our being'; but blessed is he in whom He is, who lives for Him, and is moved by Him.

"You will ask, then, since its ways are past finding out, how I know it is present? It is quick and powerful; and as soon as it has entered, it has awakened my sleeping soul, moving and softening and piercing my heart, which was in a torpor and hard as a stone. And it rooted and pulled down, to build and to plant, to water what was dry, enlighten what was dark, inflame what was cold, at the same time making the crooked way straight and the rough ways smooth, so that my soul might bless the Lord and all that is within me bless his holy name. And so it is that the Bridegroom Word, entering me at different times, has not made its entrance known by any signs, or voice, or appearance, or footstep. By no movement of its own is it manifested to me, by none of my senses does it penetrate within me; I have known its presence only by the beating of my heart, as I have just said, and I have discovered the power of its virtue by the sudden departure of vices. . . .

"But when the Word has departed, just as if you should take away the fire from beneath a boiling pot, all these things immediately begin to lie torpid and drooping; and this is to me the sign of its withdrawal. Then my soul is sad and depressed until it shall return and my heart grow warm within me, as it does, which is the indication to me that it has come back again."

Such a description does not accord with the highest mysticism, which is a clarity untouched by warmth or cold, and we have no reason to suppose that Bernard ever experienced that. But the experience described above gave him all the authority he needed to become the most powerful teacher of his age – although at least some of his popularity was due to the extraordinary magnetic power he emanated. Indeed his very charisma was in some ways his own undoing. He was in constant demand and his absence from Clairvaux became the rule rather than the exception. He longed to remain at Clairvaux in simplicity with his monks, for whom he felt great affection, but increasingly he was called upon to solve the problems of the Church. Yet at the same time his Order grew and he seems to have had a remarkably keen understanding of how his monks felt, so that even when he was away his presence seemed to stay. Clairvaux was unique. It was difficult to persuade monks to leave in order to become abbots elsewhere and frequently Bernard had to reassure them that however far away they went they would return to Clairvaux to die. Yet in spite of all his growing influence and popularity, he remained essentially humble and was frequently annoyed at being praised. He wrote to a friend: "You implore me to instruct you how to live. Fine sort of doctor, incomparable teacher that I am, who when I begin to teach what I do not know may then be expected to realise at last that I know nothing at all! A sheep might as well come to a goat for wool as you to me for guidance. . . ."

More and more Bernard became involved in the intricate politics of the day. His gifts of persuasion were so potent and purity of motive so certain that he was constantly being asked to intervene in both Church and State affairs. Consequently he became one of the most powerful figures of his time. His lightest word was listened to with respect in Rome and throughout Europe. There was hardly a reform that he did not take part in. Needless to say, this brought him enemies, particularly as he was as outspoken to strangers as he was to his friends. One day he received a letter from his friend, Cardinal Haimeric, asking him to stop interfering with the world and to stay in his own monastery. Taking this in very good part, Bernard replied: "I am vexed at having been embroiled in these disputes, especially as I know that I was not personally concerned. I am vexed but I am dragged into them none the less. But by whom can I better hope to be believed of all this than by you, the best of men?"

So he stayed peacefully at home in obedience to the Cardinal's order, but even so was not allowed to stay there for long. In 1130 the incredible news reached Clairvaux that two Popes were claiming the ascendancy and that both were willing to wage war to get what they wanted. Bernard could not hold back; it seemed the whole Church was in danger. After due consideration, he put all his energy behind Pope Innocent II, travelling with him, persuading and preaching all over France and Italy, and eventually succeeding in installing him in Rome. But the trouble was that while Bernard, by his mere presence, was able to restore order and to shame men into proper behaviour, as soon as he was gone their battles broke out again. So he was constantly back and forth, settling first one incident and then another. It was eight weary years before he was able to return to his beloved Clairvaux in peace, during which time he had travelled through much of Europe, settling quarrels, putting doubts at rest and rousing the slothful. He had managed to bring the Emperor to see the error of his ways and persuaded the King of England to support the Pope.

With some reason we might regard Bernard, as the Cardinal did, as over-active and over-zealous, particularly when we learn that he supported – indeed it was because of him that it got off the ground at all – one of the Crusades against Islam. It was a Crusade which failed, with much loss of life, and many blamed Bernard for the whole disgraceful venture. That he genuinely believed that the holy city of Jerusalem must be saved from the heathens and that this act of liberation would offer a unique opportunity to the whole Christian army to save their souls, can be raised in his defence. Also that his whole ancestry was one of soldiering. But by and large that savage event has detracted from his popularity even up to today.

And yet this is also the man who rose superbly to the defence of the Jews in Mainz, when a monk called Rudolf had inflamed the anger of the populace against them. The people, maddened by excitement, had massacred the Jews wherever they could find them, and burnt their houses to the ground. As soon as he heard, Bernard wrote at once to the Archbishop of Mainz: "Do not allow the Jews to be harmed nor speak to them except with kindness; for they are the bone and flesh of the Messiah; and if you molest them you are in danger of wounding the Lord in the apple of his eye. . . ." Rudolf was removed, and the Jews of that district still remember Bernard's protection of them with gratitude.

Any man of such burning intensity as Bernard is likely to arouse hostile criticism of all sorts, including intellectual fury. One episode has always been held against him by many scholars even up to the present. This was his total triumph over Peter Abelard, another very popular teacher of the day. There is no doubt that Bernard loved a good fight if the cause seemed just and for some time he had looked on the advanced opinions of Abelard with dislike and had openly spoken against them. But he was taken aback when, in the spring of 1141, Abelard challenged him to what amounted to an intellectual duel – to a public disputation to defend his opinions.

Abelard's teaching was new and adventurous in that it

undermined the old theology by holding it up to reason. He hoped to find what was real in Christianity without relying on faith and so he looked at the religion from the outside, as it were, holding it up to the light as though it were an object. This was incomprehensible to Bernard, for to him Biblical theology was life itself and life was the Word of God, and neither could be viewed in such a detached way – a way which seemed to him to destroy faith. Then, too, Abelard, as well as deriding the old masters, used a new terminology. "Everything has been put quite differently from what we are accustomed to hearing" grumbled the ageing Bernard. Abelard was not ageing and he was a romantic figure with a charisma of his own. He had caught the imagination of the young and they flocked to hear him give voice to his radical ideas.

Bernard seems to have been taken off balance by the whole Abelard situation – by his popularity and by his doctrines. He did not want to confront Abelard publicly, feeling that the mysteries of God were not to be disputed in this fashion. But Abelard had announced to everyone that there was to be a confrontation in Sens, on an occasion when the King of France and most of the bishops would be there to meet on Church affairs, and Bernard could not honourably get out of it. When he arrived he found the city decked out as though for a carnival and the handsome Abelard moving among the crowds with his admirers. Grey, gaunt and weak – for he was perpetually ill – Bernard must have felt himself badly out of place in such a gathering.

On the next day he attended the formal meeting of the Council in the cathedral. He read aloud from Abelard's works the passages which he considered objectionable and then called on Abelard to defend them. But to everyone's amazement, Abelard, who had been so full of confidence and determination, refused to reply. "I will not answer the Cistercian" he said. "I appeal to Rome."

No real reason has ever been discovered why Abelard should have suddenly backed out in this way. He had arranged the meeting himself and was surrounded by friends and supporters. For some reason – and critics of Bernard suggest that he had already influenced the Council against Abelard and that Abelard knew this – he lost courage at the last moment. In the event all his works went to Rome, as he requested, but they were condemned and his books publicly burnt and he himself given the discipline of spending the rest of his life in a monastery. He happened to be at Cluny when he heard the news. He stayed on and was reconciled with Bernard before dying two years later – some say of a broken heart.

Bernard himself died in 1153. He had been a sick man all his life, probably fighting tuberculosis as well as chronic gastric complaints, but he never allowed himself to become an invalid and lived energetically into his sixties. He died of 'a fever'. So great was the esteem in which he was held that a mere twenty years passed before he was canonised.

We may not see him in quite that saintly light. The extremes he went to were perhaps too violent, the barbed and caustic tongue often too sharp, the politician too much in the way of the holy man. Yet his teaching was in many ways excellent and one thing we can never doubt – he loved God, the Reality of his life, utterly, and was prepared to sacrifice himself without measure in God's service.

"Saw ye whom my soul loves? O swift, vehement, burning, impetuous love, who suffers no other thought than of you, scorns all things else, condemns all things save you, content with yourself! You confound rules, conceal usage, know not any measure; all that seems to belong to opportunity, to reason, to reticence, to counsel or to judgement – that you triumph over in yourself and reduce to captivity."

Richard Rolle

Such a passionate surrender as Bernard's was echoed by Richard Rolle, author of *The Fire of Love* – although Yorkshire in the early part of the fourteenth century was largely illiterate in contrast with Bernard's eloquent France. Knowledge of Christianity in most of rural England came at that time from visual aids such as stained-glass windows or wall paintings, from the talk of passing friars, and from the parish priest. Frequently the local church was under the wing of a monastery, which granted a small wage to the priest and took the rest of the income. This meant that only the poor were prepared to take on the duties of parish priest, and since there were few facilities for training them, many priests were as ignorant and superstitious as their flock. Sermons were rare, and slight in content.

But the people of this dynamic century were filled with a spirit of enquiry and flocked to hear the preaching of the wandering friars. Everyone was aware of the big gulf between the wretchedly poor parish priests and friars, and the rich, worldly monks and bishops, and a strong anti-ecclesiastical feeling was growing – echoing the rest of Europe. People remembered that the lands and wealth which the Church enjoyed had been donated by pious laymen and there was a rebellious feeling that what had once been given might be taken back if misused. There was also deep resentment over the tithes which the Church extracted.

Except for Border fights with the Scots, England then was at peace and thriving. It was an age of colour, drama, and miracles. Everyone took part in processions and festivals, music and mime. Wandering players came to the villages, and on such great popular festivals as May Day and Midsummer Day a whole village would give itself up to mirth and dance. Much of it was crude, especially on such occasions as weddings and funerals (the Church frowned ineffectively on the feasting and drinking and consequent merriment which went on at funerals), but above all it was an age of strong individualism, and of deep searching, particularly among the middle classes, for a true sense of the God-ground.

Into this setting was born Richard Rolle, who carried in his character the strong independence which marks him out from the other mystics in this book. He is the odd one out, the nonconforming, who never went to church any more than he had to but who loved God and his 'merry Jesus' in single-minded adoration all his life.

Richard was the earliest of the fourteenth-century group of English mystics, which included Julian of Norwich, the author of the *Cloud*, and Walter Hilton, and he is often called the father of English mysticism. There was a particular homeliness and realism about this group – perhaps we see it most clearly in Mother Julian – which seemed to carry a strong urge to *love* God rather than to think him. It was a freer religion of the heart than much of its continental counterpart, with tenderness and happiness shining through. It was devotional, adoring, passionate and joyful, full of imagery, colour and poetry. Above all it was fresh with originality.

Richard himself was not a philosopher, unlike the author of the *Cloud*. He wanted most of all to *experience* the spiritual life and because of this he turned away from intellectual pursuits altogether – although, ironically, he is also known as the father of English literature, since he wrote beautifully and his works were circulated all over England and Europe during the fourteenth and fifteenth centuries. He preceded Wycliff by a few years and had already translated some of the psalms as well as writing many of his own thoughts in English by the time Wycliff came to translate the Bible. Indeed when Wycliff started this mammoth task he found ready to hand Richard Rolle's translation and commentary upon the psalms and canticles, and it is believed that he based his English version on these. But the reputation of Wycliff, the great reformer, writer and contentious 'heretic', has always eclipsed that of Rolle.

Richard Rolle was born in Yorkshire and lived most of his life in its dales. His birth coincided with the new century – he was probably born in 1300. His father, William, seems to have been of moderately good family although by no means rich. No childhood stories of Richard survive, but it is known that he was intelligent and bright as a young boy and hoped then to follow a scholar's way of life. With the kind help of Thomas de Neville, Archdeacon of Durham, he was sent to Oxford. He was then fourteen.

At that time England was divided more by language than by anything else. Each county, particularly in the Midlands and North, had its own strong dialect amounting almost to a native tongue which was virtually incomprehensible elsewhere – particularly in the South where Norman French was still common. When Richard arrived at Oxford, one of the greatest scholarly centres of Europe, the medley of foreign tongues must have confused the young boy, while at the same time few people were able to understand his speech. However, scholar's Latin was a bridge between broad Yorkshire and the supple talk of southerners and no doubt Richard was able to hold his own. Yet for a boy brought up in a small village (Thornton-le-Dale) in North Yorkshire the Oxford scene must have been bewildering and often overwhelming. Let us hope it fascinated him as well, for undoubtedly it was full of life and drama. To quote from the *Quarterly Review* of January 1892:

"Within the walls of the city – in the narrow, ill-paved, dirty streets which, overhung by signs, wound through rows of tall, irregularly-built houses ... were herded together a motley throng, over which neither chancellor nor mayor ... could exercise any control. The rough upland folks occupied the centre of the streets with their carts and strings of pack-horses. At the sides crowded citizens in every dress, plying their various trades, ready to promote a riot by pelting a scholar with offal from the butcher's stall, prompt to draw their knives at a moment's notice. Here moved to and fro among the shops and stalls, Jews in their yellow gaberdines, black Benedictines and white Cistercians; friars black, white and grey; men-at-arms from the castle; flocks of lads of twelve to fourteen, who had entered some grammar school or religious house to pass the first stage of the university course. Here passed a group of ragged, gaunt, yellow-visaged sophisters, returning peacefully from lectures to their inns, but

with their 'bastards', or daggers, as well as their leather
pouches at their waists. Here a knot of students fantastically
attired in many-coloured garments . . . wearing beards, long
hair, furred cloaks, and shoes chequered with red and green,
paraded through the thoroughfare, heated with wine from the
feast of some graduating bachelor. Here a line of servants
carrying the books of scholars or of doctors to the schools, or
there a procession of colleagues escorting to the grave the body
of some master, and bearing before the corpse a silver cross,
threaded the throng. . . . Here gleamed a mantle of crimson
cloth, symbolising the blood of the Saviour, or the budge-
edged hood of a doctor of law or of theology, for it was then an
ambition to wear, not to evade, the academic dress. In the
hubbub of voices which proceeded from this miscellaneous,
parti-coloured mob, might be distinguished every accent,
every language and every dialect. A medieval university was
essentially cosmopolitan, and the influx of foreigners into
Oxford was very great, especially when the University of Paris
was temporarily dispersed and when the Franciscan schools
were at the height of their reputation. Frenchmen, Germans,
Spaniards, jostled in the streets against English, Scots, Irish
and Welsh; Kentish students mingled with students from
Somerset or Yorkshire, and the speech of each was unin-
telligible to the other. National hostilities, clan hatreds, local
jealousies, intellectual antipathies, differences of blood,
language and race, contributed to the heterogeneous character
of the university. Men of the same nationality, province or
county, congregated together, advanced under their own
distinguishing banners to the fray, and in celebrations of the
festivals of their own patron saints found more fruitful
occasions of brawling than in football or cudgel-playing.

"What fires there were, were of charcoal or wood. There
were no chimneys, and the smoke had to escape by a hole in the
roof. The streets had no sidewalks and were either of mud or
cobbled; open streams and gutters, called kennels, running
through them which were used as receptacles for every sort of
refuse, either thrown from the windows above or from the
stalls of the market-sellers. The shambles alone in that
crowded 'Row' must have been cause enough for many
plagues. . . ."

There is no record of how things went for Richard in these conditions, but they would not be altogether strange to him. Nevertheless an impression is given from his writings that he detested Oxford. His nature was a solitary one, his birthplace quiet and peaceful. He had gone to Oxford because he was gifted with a good brain and it was expected that he would do well – most likely in the Church. But long before the end of his seven-year course he gave it all up and went home.

He was eighteen or nineteen. He had come to a crisis-point in his life, realising that all the theological disputations, the philosophising, the scholastic arguments over words and doctrinal points, were to him hopelessly far from the real life of the spirit. He no longer wanted to use his intellect for mere knowledge. It is probable that he was fired in this by the teaching of William of Ockham (that same William who shared detention with Eckhart in Avignon and who escaped to teach again). In the great debates of the day, Ockham, an ardent Franciscan friar of an evangelical nature, taught a personal burning love for Christ which undoubtedly Richard responded to with all his nature. Ockham also taught independence of mind – indeed his imprisonment at Avignon had been because he openly flouted papal authority and supported the cause of Louis of Bavaria against Pope John XXII. The fact of the great schism – two rival popes opposing each other – must have caused a vast stir in Oxford where undoubtedly sides were taken. No doubt Richard threw himself into the fight as much as any other boy, but no doubt also his more thoughtful nature seized on the independence of Ockham, his refusal to submit to the Church, and his adventurous personal path of devotion to Jesus.

For Richard intended to follow this path too. He longed to know God rather than about what God was like – he wanted to experience the actual Reality and we can easily understand how barren and frustrating the scholastic debates and arguments were to him. In fact his books bristle with hostility towards the subtleties of the schoolmen. In *The Fire of Love* he speaks of "those taught by knowledge gotten, not inborn, and puffed up with inflated arguments who are disdainful, saying: where learned he? who read to him? for they do not believe that the lovers of endless love might be taught by their inward Master to speak better than those taught by men, who have studied at all times for vain honours''.

Later he was to expand on this when he stated that God can only be known through love and not through knowledge:

"You ask what God is? I answer you shortly: such a one and so great is He that none other is or ever may be like Him or so great. If you want to talk about what God is, I say that you shall never find an answer to this question. I have not known; angels know not; archangels have not heard. Wherefore how would you know what is unknown and also unteachable?

"Yet also it is good to know God perfectly; that is to say, he cannot be conceived by the mind, but knowing Him is to love Him; loving Him to sing in Him; singing to rest in Him; and by inward rest to come to endless rest. Let it not disturb you that I have said to know God perfectly and I have denied that He may be known, since the prophet in the psalm has said: 'Show them Thy mercy who knew Thee. . . .' He truly knows God perfectly that feels Him incomprehensible and unable to be known."

Perfect knowledge, then, cannot be found through speculation but only through intuition and love. It cannot be shaped into form by scholarly learning but must follow its own intrinsic path – "Truly they [the independent contemplatives] are like the stone that is called topaz which is seldom found and therefore is held most precious and full dear, in which are found two colours; one is most pure even as gold, and the other clear as heaven when it is right. And it overcomes all the clearness of all the stones; and nothing is fairer to behold. But if any would polish it, it is made dim, and truly if it is left to itself its clearness is retained."

This insight into the nature of spiritual truth was to take Richard some years to discover. In the meantime he forsook Oxford and, in a mood of high exhilaration and dedication, returned home. When he first arrived back at Thornton-le-Dale, no doubt his father and the Archdeacon were disappointed and even angry at his unfinished career. His next actions were surprising and we shall never know the reasons for them except that there might have been a feeling of soreness at being misunderstood which entered into his new-found zeal.

For shortly after he got back, he left again, and this time

finally. In a melodramatic gesture (we must remember that he was only nineteen) he decided that his life from then on was to be that of a hermit and consequently he should *look* like one. He persuaded his sister to bring two of her dresses, a grey and white, to a small wood near the house. He then cut off the sleeves from the grey dress, stripped, put on the white dress with its flowing upper sleeves, and then slipped the grey tunic over it. He placed his father's rainhood on his head, presumably as a cowl, and emerged from the trees. At the sight of this apparition, his sister was horrified. "My brother is mad! My brother is mad!" she shouted. Her cries were so loud that Richard was afraid he would be caught and dragged back to the house so he took to his heels and ran. It was in this way that his hermit's life began.

He ran and walked all day across the moors, having, as he said, 'fled that which confused me', and at evening reached a small church about twenty-four miles from his home. He was full of fervour and otherworldliness, aware that he had now committed himself to what seemed to him a most wonderful life, one in which he put himself completely in the hands of God. Underhill comments that he ran away to God as other boys run away to sea, and his whole life must then have appeared to him full of adventure, hope and freedom. On that first evening, when he reached the little church, he went in and knelt down to pray on a stool in front of the burning lamp. He became so lost in his prayer that he did not notice when the lady of the manor came in. He was kneeling where she usually knelt and he would have been removed had she not signalled that she would not have him disturbed. She was touched by the depth of his devotion and perhaps amused, although sympathetically, by his strange garments. After the service, when Richard stood up, her sons recognised him as a fellow student at Oxford.

It is not known where he spent that night, but it was probably in the church. On the following morning, still filled with high exaltation, and without being asked, he clothed himself in a spare surplice and sang matins with the congregation. Later at mass, this time with the consent of the priest, he mounted the pulpit and delivered the sermon of his life – one in which he poured out his love for Jesus and his devotion to a

God-filled life. It is said that the congregation were so moved that they wept.

But afterwards he suffered the inevitable reaction to any great 'high' and found himself shy and timid once more. His wonderful new life seemed barren and he saw himself more as a truant than as a wandering hermit. But the squire was touched by his plight and asked him to dinner. In somewhat arrogant fashion (unfortunately typical of Richard, who was never an altogether endearing man) he took himself off to an unused attic because – as Richard Misyn, his biographer, tells us – he wanted to fulfil the teaching of the Gospel which says: 'When you are invited to a wedding, sit down in the lowest room; that when he that bade thee cometh, he may say unto thee, Friend, go up higher.' Richard was able to fulfil this command, but only because the good squire looked for him everywhere and, having at last found him in the attic, did in fact put him next to him at the dinner table, which meant he was above the squire's sons. But Richard said not a single word throughout the meal and with singular lack of manners, as soon as he had eaten enough, he got up to go. Then the squire told him this was not customary and sat him down again until the meal was ended. Once more he got up to leave but this time the squire, John Dalton, stated firmly that he wanted to talk to him in private. When everyone else had gone he began to question Richard. He was the most kindly of men and, with sons of his own, no doubt had much sympathy for Richard. As well, he was a warm friend of Richard's father. He asked Richard if William Rolle was his father and Richard reluctantly answered that he was. He must have felt himself in a very awkward position because he had run away to be a hermit without his father's knowledge or consent. Nevertheless John Dalton treated him more than well: "And when the aforesaid squire had examined him in private, and convinced himself by perfect evidence of the sanctity of his purpose, he, at his own expense, clad him according to his wish with clothing suitable for a hermit; and kept him for a long time in his own house, giving him a place for his solitary abode and providing him with food and all the necessaries of life."

Dalton no doubt had the discernment to see the genuine longing beneath the youthful awkwardness and the actor's costume. And indeed it is evident that in all ages there are young men and women who feel a burning call to commit themselves to causes and to ways of life which do not accord with their parents' wishes for them. In our own day we have watched the young dress as Sufis, Hare Krishnas, Buddhist monks, orange Rajneesh followers and dreaming flower people. We have also seen them become Evangelical Christians who are 'born again'; and take on the celibate and committed life of the Moonies, following a no-drink, no-drugs, no-war programme for the sake of a new world. In America hysterical parents pay large sums of money for strong-arm men to kidnap their own children back and 'de-programme' them. For what reason? How much better surely to look beneath the youthful absurdities, as John Dalton did, and to give them all that is possible in the way of help and support?

For some time Richard remained in the Dalton household and was looked after by them. Then it appears that he went off to a lonelier part of the Dalton estate. It was during these first years, however, that he had mystical experiences and began to write and teach.

In *The Fire of Love* he tells us what happened to him: "I was sitting in the chapel and while I was much delighted with the sweetness of meditation, suddenly I felt within me a merry and unknown heat. At first I wondered about it, for a long time doubting what it could be. I was sure that it was not from a creaturely cause, but from my Maker, because I found it grew hotter and more glad."

This feeling of heat came to him 'three years except for three or four months' from the time he left home (he is very exact with his timing and quite objective about his experiences), and it remained with him for nearly a year, until the next experience occurred:

"Truly, in this unexpected and sweet-smelling heat, half a year, three months and some weeks have passed – until this new incoming and receiving of a heavenly and spiritual sound, which belongs without time or place to songs of worship and the sweetness of unseen melody; because it can only be known by him who has separated himself from the world.

"While I sat in the same chapel, singing psalms in the night before supper, I seemed to hear above me the noise as it were of readers, or rather singers. And while I prayed to heaven with my whole heart, suddenly, I cannot tell in what manner, I felt in me the noise of song and received the most enchanting heavenly melody which stayed with me in my mind. And then my thought was changed to a constant song of mirth, and praises came into my meditation and into my prayers and psalm-saying. I gave out the same sound as I heard from then on, with a feeling of great inward sweetness. I burst out singing what before I had said, but only in private and alone before my Maker. Nothing was known by them that saw me, for if they had known it they would have honoured me too much and so I would have lost part of the most fair flower and should have felt forsaken.

"In the meantime wonder caught me that I should be taken up to so great a mirth while I was still solitary; and that God should give such gifts to me, ones that I knew not even what to ask for and that I could hardly believe that any man, even the holiest, could receive in this life. Therefore I believe that this is not given for any special reason, but freely to whom Christ will; nevertheless I also believe no man receives it unless he specially loves the name of Jesus, and honours it so much that he never lets it pass from his mind except in sleep."

The repeating of the name of Jesus is a spiritual practice going back to the Desert Fathers and far beyond. It is a world-wide technique for calming the mind and bringing it to a one-pointed clarity. The Greek Church uses the technique to this day and it is given full honour in the *Philokalia*, its collection of spiritual writings. Richard himself says: "If you would stand well with God, and have grace to rule your life and come to the joy of love, this name JESUS, fasten it so in your heart that it is never lost from your thought. And when you speak to him, and through custom say Jesus, it shall be in your ear joy; in your mouth honey, and in your heart melody: for men shall think joy to hear that name named, sweetness to speak it, mirth and song to think it. If you think on Jesus continually, and hold it firmly, it purges your sin and kindles your heart; it clarifies your soul, it removes anger and does away with stupidity. It wounds in love and fulfils in charity; it chases the devil and puts out dread; it opens heaven and makes a contemplative man. . . ."

Later he added: "One thing I counsel you: that you should not forget the name IHESU, but think it in your heart night and day as your special-dear treasure. Love It more than life, root It in your mind. Love Ihesu for he made you and bought you full dearly. Give your heart to him for it is in his debt. Therefore set your love on his name Ihesu, that is Heal. There will be no sick thing dwelling in the heart when Ihesu is held truly in the mind."

What the name meant to Rolle personally he describes in the *Fire*:

"Until the time I can clearly see my Beloved, I shall think of his full sweet Name, holding it, joying, in my mind. For it is no marvel that he is happy in this life who longs to fulfil the desire of his Maker. Nothing is merrier than Jesu to sing, nothing more delightful that Jesu to hear. Hearing truly fills the mind with mirth, and song uplifts it. And truly, while I still long for this, sighing, and heavy as it were with hunger and thirst, I think myself forsaken. But when I feel the embrace and kissing of my love, with untold delight I overflow; and true lovers, for love only of his unmeasured goodness, put this before all things. Coming therefore into me, he comes inshedding perfect love. My heart also he refreshes, giving it perseverance. He warms me and makes me fat, all the leanness of longing put away."

This then was Richard's practice; and heat, sweetness and song were his experiences. He is unusual, although not alone, in hearing melody; and the song which poured forth from him in place of speech was an exultant and adoring prayer. The true lover, he says, "has sweetness, heat and spiritual song and by this he serves God and draws close to Him. Sometimes he feels more of heat and sweetness and sings with difficulty, sometimes truly with great sweetness he is ravished, when heat is felt the less; often also he flees and passes into heavenly song with great mirth, and also he knows the heat and sweetness of love are with him. Nevertheless heat is never without sweetness, although sometimes it is without song."

What in fact did Rolle mean by heat, sweetness and song? In our day it is easy to dismiss such experiences and there are several ways in which we can do so. We can think of his long hours of solitude, usually kneeling or sitting and probably with a scanty diet lacking in protein, and we can say that this was imagination and delusion. Or we can apply a psychological term and call it auto-hypnotism, or a medical term, when it is psycho-physical hallucination. In psychical language we can say that it is induced sense-automatism. Or we can go one better than all of those descriptions and point out that on the religious path such states happen to many if not most people, that they are best paid little attention to, and that the true goal can only be discovered when they are left behind.

This last criticism has validity and should be taken seriously. Other contemporary mystics, such as Walter Hilton and the author of the *Cloud*, warn against such things. In his list of mystical automatisms, Walter Hilton mentions with much suspicion, 'sensible heat, as it were fire, glowing and warming the breast' and the author of the *Cloud* says that amongst the many delusions which come to 'young, presumptuous con-templatives' are 'many quaint heats and burnings in their bodily breasts'. The Japanese, too, have a term, *makyo*, for all the misleading psychological states and manifestations which arise during Zen training, and there is no doubt that the best religious teaching is not concerned with those states as such but in going beyond them.

But let us suppose that we do not take their advice, nor bother with any of the other dismissive terms mentioned, but with a clear and concept-free mind make ourselves available to Rolle on *his* terms, listening to him on *his* wavelength and not that of any other authority. What do we find? We find that what happened to Rolle seemed absolutely real and had immense meaning. For instance, about heat he says: "So burning and gladdening that he or she who is in this degree can feel the fire of love burning in their soul as well as you can feel your finger burn if you put it in the fire." That is surely straightforward enough? Whatever we, who do not know it, may think about it, Rolle experienced it just as he described it. He continues:

"I have marvelled more than I ever showed when I first felt my heart wax warm, *truly, and not in imagination*, but as if it were burned with physical fire. I was amazed as the burning in my soul burst up, and with it an unknown sense of comfort; often because of my ignorance of such abundant heat, I have groped around my chest seeking whether this burning was from my skin or any outward cause. But when I knew that it was kindled inwardly from a spiritual cause, and that this burning was nothing to do with the flesh, in this I conceived it was the gift of my Maker. Gladly therefore am I melted into the longing for greater love; and especially for the inflowing of that most sweet delight and intangible sweetness, the which, with that burning flame, has comforted my mind to its very core."

Such graphic descriptions of the effect of heat leave us in no doubt that what Rolle experienced was not imagination. How then about sweetness? Once more this is an area where body, mind and 'soul' (individuality) cannot be separated. What the 'soul' experiences through the mind, the body feels. When we are happy our whole body feels light and alive, when we are sad it droops and feels heavy. True spiritual insights are often accompanied by a lightening or enlightening of the whole person so that there is a general feeling of full accord and integration in an atmosphere of greater reality. And there is a tendency to smiles and laughter as the tensions disappear, so that Rolle's constant use of the word 'mirth' is fully right and justified – a word which he explains by saying that laughter which comes from a clear conscience and from a free spirit is to be praised – "the which is only in the righteous, and it is called mirth in the love of God". So there is no need to disbelieve Rolle when he talks of sweetness as 'a sweet mystery' or 'a marvellous honey'. "With what labour it is got," he says, "but with what untold joy it is possessed."

Such happiness is even extolled by the scrupulously practical author of the *Cloud*. He says: "Sometimes He will enflame the body of His devout servants here in this life: not once or twice but as often as He likes, with full wonderful sweetness and comforts. Of which some are not coming into this body from without, but are from within; rising and springing in an abundance of ghostly gladness, and of true devotion. Such a comfort and such a sweetness should not be suspected: and I believe that he that feels it should not doubt it."

Rolle's melody, to those of us who love music but are not musical, can only be a matter of wonder and envy. He seems to have heard it first outside and then inside his mind. It was as real to him as any vision is to those who 'see' rather than 'hear'.

Rolle was by nature a musician and a poet and his intense rapture of joy and love found its expression in the lyrical poems which he wrote and sang. "O good Jesu, my heart you have bound in thought of your Name, and now I cannot but sing it." He sang everything – his prayers, his thoughts, his meditations. Of contemplation, he says: "If it be asked, 'What is contemplation?' it is hard to define. Some say contemplative life is a knowledge of the unknown, or a study of God's words . . . or it is freedom to see through the visioned truth of wisdom, lit up with a full high marvel. Others say that it is a free and wise insight into the greatness of the soul, others again that it is the death of fleshly desire. But to me it seems that contemplation is the joyful singing of God's love, taken into the mind with the sweetness of angels' praises."

So fond was he of the melody which came to him inwardly that he found it hard to attend church services and take part in what seemed a more clumsy form of song. For this he was severely criticised – "they stood up against me because I fled the outward songs that are used in the churches, and the sweetness of the organ that is gladly heard by the people, and only going there when the need of hearing mass – which elsewhere I could not hear – or the solemnity of the day asked it."

It was in this spirit that he dedicated his book, *The Fire of Love*, "Not to philosophers nor wise men of this world, nor to great divines lapped in infinite questions, but to the boisterous and untaught, more busy to learn to love God than to know many things; for truly, working rather than disputing is to know and love. I believe that the things contained in this book will not be understood by those questioners who are in all science most high in learning but in the love of God most low."

It need not be hard then for most of us who have never experienced either 'heat' or 'sweetness' or 'melody', or the visions which were also very common in medieval times, to make the breakthrough – in sympathetic understanding at least – to that level of Reality where they are experienced. And indeed in this world of mysteries, not the least of which is its own existence, why should we question that there are some which it is not in our nature to experience? We all approach the centre of our being by different paths according to our own individuality. Rolle himself was well aware of this:

"As the works of saints are different, so are their meditations different. Yet all, because they arise from one source, go to one end, and lead to one bliss . . . therefore the psalm says: 'He has led me upon the paths of righteousness', as if to say there is one righteousness and many paths by which we are led to its joy; because while we are one in our being, we are many in our needs. . . . God sheds forth good thoughts and meditations to each one as best accords their state and condition. So I can tell you my meditations but which is most effective for *you* I cannot say for I do not see your inward desires. I believe truly that those meditations which bring you the most profit please God the most, and he by his mercy sheds them in you."

Nevertheless there *is* a difference between the 'young presumptuous contemplatives' (which today might include those who go in for drug-induced hallucinations) and the states which are the by-products of a breakthrough into Reality itself. It was not for nothing that 'two years, three months and some weeks' passed before Rolle received any of these gifts. All that time had been spent in an unremitting effort to abandon himself to God. This had involved overcoming all his natural sensual desires. Quite a task for a young man in his early twenties. But the essence of that task was not so much in repressive bodily austerities – indeed he had much common sense in that regard – as in 'contrition of thought, and pulling out of desires that do not belong to loving or worshipping God'. So it was a programme of learning to be humble and simple that he set himself. In one of his most beautiful passages he refers to that beginning:

"In the beginning of my conversion and singular purpose, I thought I would be like the little bird that for love of her lover longs, but in her longing she is gladdened when he comes whom she loves. And joying she sings, and singing she longs, but in sweetness and heat. It is said the nightingale is given to song and melody all night, that she may please him to whom she is joined. How much more with greatest sweetness to Christ my Jesu should I sing, who is spouse of my soul in this present life – which is night in regard to the clearness to come."

Some self-mortification was inevitable to one of Richard's

nature, and because he was so young he may have over-dramatised his 'sins'. From what he writes, he was no celibate by nature but some 'sin' he had committed, probably at Oxford, seemed to haunt him. He begs God to have mercy on him for 'my youth was fond; my childhood vain; my young age unclean'. Elsewhere he resolves 'to expiate the sin which as a boy I had committed'. He also talks of a young woman, the same whom he had sinned against, coming into his dreams at the beginning of his new life and how he then cast her out. He thanks God that it begins to feel sweet to forgo worldly pleasures and says: "But now, Lord Jesu, my heart is enflamed with Your holy love and my reins are changed." But they were not changed overnight. He tells us of what must have been a humiliating lesson:

"Nevertheless now, lately, from three worthy women I received a deserved reproof." Apparently he had been involved in horseplay with them in too rough a fashion and with too much familiarity. "The fourth woman, to whom I was in part familiar [she was probably part of the Dalton household] not reproving but as it were despising me, said: 'You have nothing but fair looks and fair words, of good deeds you have none.'"

Food too he was fond of but had the sense to see that neither extreme of too much or too little (as in St Bernard's case) was the right answer: "In meat and drink be scarce and wise. While you eat and drink do not let the memory of your God that feeds you pass from your mind; but praise, bless and glorify Him in every morsel, so that your soul is not parted from God at any time. Doing this shall make you worthy, and the temptations of the fiend, that in meat and drink awaits most men and beguiles them, shall not tempt you. Either by immoderate taking of food are such men thrown down from virtue or by too much abstinence they break down in virtue too.

"There are always those who fluctuate in eating, so that they always take too little or too much; and they can never keep the right form of living while they believe that now this, now that, is better. The unwise and untaught, who never felt the sweetness of Christ's love, believe that unwise abstinence is holiness; and they believe they cannot be worthy of much in God's eyes unless they are the most singular of men in scarceness and unrighteous abstinence. . . . The best thing, and as I suppose the most pleasing to God, is to adapt yourself in meat and drink to the time and place and station of those whom you are with; so that you do not seem to be wilful nor pretending to be holy."

Such sound advice from the young man who once hid in an attic! It parallels the Buddha's 'middle way'. But it is in his actual methods of contemplation that we come to unusual aspects of Rolle's understanding. He found, he said, that sitting was to him the best posture in which to contemplate, better then kneeling or moving about.

"For if I tried to contemplate while standing, walking or lying, I thought that I lacked a great deal in myself and seemed to myself desolate; because of this, and constrained by the need that I should live in great devotion, I chose to sit. The cause of this I know well; for if a man stands or walks for some time, his body waxes weary and so the soul is limp, and in a manner feels itself a load, and he is not in true quietness and so, it follows, not in true mindfulness. For the soul is made wise by rest or sitting. He that is more delighted in God standing than sitting, may know that he is full far from the height of contemplation."

This last remark is unnecessary, since it seems over-dogmatic to assert that one cannot contemplate standing up. Unfortunately Rolle tended to consider his own ways the best and this slight arrogance may have been one result of living entirely on his own, independent of monasteries or orders of hermits – where discussion might have refined his views – although there were many such in Yorkshire at the time.

As for the rest, though, sitting meditation is undoubtedly the great technique of our age and it is interesting to find that Rolle understood its value in those days. Its benefits are very real if the body does not sag but stays straight to allow good breathing, and if the head does not loll but rests comfortably on the neck so that there is no tendency to doze but rather a state of alertness and receptiveness. The object of zazen (sitting meditation), for instance, is to ensure that the moving, wavering everyday mind is quietened and the perpetual commentator silenced so that a calm and clear mind, able to see the reality of things, can take its place. The interaction of body and mind is self-evident from our own observation, and as Philip Kapleau points out, a bent back "deprives the mind of its tension so that it is quickly invaded by random thoughts and images, but a straight back by strengthening concentration lessens the incidence of wandering thoughts . . . this is not to imply, however, that zazen cannot be practised unless one sits in the full or half lotus posture. Zazen can in fact be effective even in a chair or on a bench or while kneeling, provided the back is straight. In the last resort what ensures success in the quest for enlightenment is not a particular posture but an intense longing for truth for its own sake, which alone leads one to sit regularly in any fashion and to perform all the affairs of daily life with devotion and clear awareness.''

Echoing this passage, Patanjali, a second-century Indian yogi who brought together all the teachings of yoga into a famous book of aphorisms, states in verse form:

> This is the beginning of instruction in yoga.
> Yoga is the control of thought-waves in the mind.
> Then man abides in his real nature.
> At other times man remains identified with the
>   thought waves.

In Rolle's words: "In what state may men love God the most? I answer in such state as it be that men are most in rest of body and soul, and least occupied with any needs or business of this world. For the thought of love of Jesus Christ and of that infinite joy – that thought always looks for outward rest so that it shall not be hindered by comers and goers, and the occupations of worldly things; and it seeks within great silence from the annoyances of desires, and of vanities and of earthly thoughts. And especially all who love contemplative life, they seek rest in body and soul. For a great Doctor says: 'They are God's throne who dwell still in one place and are not running about, but in sweetness of Christ's love are fixed.'"

About himself he says: "I have loved to sit, not for penance or fantasy, nor that I wished men to talk of me, not for any such thing, but only because I knew that I loved God more and longer lastingly within the *comfortableness* of love, than going, standing or kneeling. For sitting I am in most rest and my heart most upwards."

For such sitting he needed solitude. He said: "He truly feels himself solitary when God is not with him. But he that chooses the solitary life *for* God, and leads it in good manner, is not near woe but great happiness; and the name of Jhesu shall continually delight his mind; and the more men are not afraid to follow a life which is without the solace of other men, the more they shall be gladdened with the comfort of God. Spiritual visitations they will often receive, which, when they were in company they knew not at all. Therefore it is said to a beloved soul, 'I shall lead her into the wilderness and there I shall speak unto her heart'."

"As when we stand in darkness," he said, "and see nothing, so in contemplation – which invisibly lights up the soul – no seen light we see. Christ also makes darkness his resting-place and speaks to us as though through a cloud. But that, when it is felt, is fully delectable. And man's love is perfect, even though his flesh prevents him seeing it, when he desires nothing but God. By this it is shown that holiness does not lie in a weeping of the heart, or tears, or outward labours, but in the sweetness of perfect compassion and heavenly contemplation. Many truly have broken down in tears and then have afterwards returned to their bad ways; but no man could be involved with worldly business when he has truly joyed in timeless love. To weep and to sorrow belong to the newly converted and the beginners; but to sing joyfully and to go forth in contemplation belongs only to the perfect.

"Contemplation is sweet and desirable labour. It gladdens the labourer and hurts not. No man can do this and not feel joyful; not when it comes, but when it goes, he feels weary. O noble and marvellous working that those who sit do most perfectly!

"Nothing is more profitable, nothing merrier, than the grace of contemplation that lifts us from all low things and offers us to God. What is this grace but the beginning of joy? And what is the perfection of joy but grace confirmed? In which is kept for us a joyful happiness and happy joy, a glorious endlessness and timeless joy; to live with the saints and dwell with the angels. And that which is above all things – truly to know God; to love him perfectly; and in the shining of his majesty to see him and, with a wonderful song of joy and melody, to praise him without end."

Rolle's personality was by nature a solitary and shy one and always, to the end of his life, he preferred aloneness to the company of others. In fact for one whose prose is so lyrical and inspired, his relationship to the outside world was strangely unhappy until the later years of his life. Only then does he seem to have acquired the inner strength of a true teacher, for in his youth and early middle age he was constantly made angry and bitter by the unkind things often said about him. He frequently refers to 'backbyttinge' during the years in which he was a wandering preacher, but one can't help feeling that he drew some of this upon himself by a clumsy approach to people and also by the fact that he was an individualist and looked to no support from the Church or a monastery. As an unordained lay preacher he was therefore unprotected, and was treated with lack of respect by both ordinary people and the Church – so much so that often he had nowhere to sleep. He speaks occasionally of the cold, of lack of clothes and of hunger.

Yet he never wavered. There must have been times when he longed for a home of his own – but instead he courageously developed his inner mind as his home through reading (mainly the Scriptures), prayer, meditation and contemplation. When he speaks of prayer, he says: "If you are in temptation or tribulation, then run to prayer. For if you pray clearly you shall have help."

There is clear evidence that when we are in real need and we ask – even blindly and with no faith – for help, it almost always comes. Sometimes it comes in ways we are not expecting; and sometimes the specific thing we have asked for may be so wrong for us that we do not get it – but in that case we get something else instead.

What is it that responds to our appeal? One can understand a belief in guardian angels, in the manifestation of one's teacher, or in the concreteness of Jesus or Krishna or Kuan Yin – for quite often there seems to be a direct intervention which we ourselves could not have accomplished.

The key seems to be in surrender. We give up, we cannot help ourselves and so we implore the Void for help. And mysteriously that surrender brings a response. But perhaps the more we attempt to analyse and elucidate this response the further away we shall remove ourselves from it.

Prayer to Rolle, in any case, was a constant and important activity and not merely for use in despair. He himself found that "When we pray well we think of no other thing, for all our mind is addressed to heaven and our soul is enflamed with the fire of the Holy Ghost. Thus a marvellous plenteousness of God's goodness is found in us; for from the innermost marrow of our hearts shall the love of God rise, and all our prayer shall be with desire and effect; so that we overrun not only the words but nearly every syllable with a great cry and desire we shall offer to our Lord. . . ."

But to those who could not pray well, he offered this advice: "Although we cannot gather our hearts together as we would yet we should not leave off, but little by little we should learn to grow in prayer, that at last Jesu Christ may make us stable in it."

We do well to heed Rolle's words. If we take prayer in a wide sense, it is communication; and to those who do not like Christological – or indeed Hebraic or Islamic – labels, we can say that it is communication with our own innermost self. For many people there is no communication with themselves at all except at a very superficial level. Their minds are full of irrelevant information which distracts them from themselves like a drug. Rolle was right. In order to communicate with ourselves we very often need solitude.

What is this communication about? Very often it is the same as the content of prayer is supposed to be. We can talk to the sea or to the wind about our deepest anxieties and stresses, our happiness or our wonder. In the most intimate detail we can communicate – wherever we are and either aloud or silently. And this communication may lead us into a new dimension of being at one with ourselves; it eases our hearts; and it draws us towards being one with the world too, not estranged from it. For when contact and communication with the depths of ourselves occurs in a direct and spontaneous way, we no longer think in subjective or objective terms and there seems no separation between ourselves and all other forms of existence. Inner prayer, for Rolle, was to Jesus. To us it may be to That which is.

Rolle was still a young man and his attitudes to prayer as yet barely formed when he left the Dalton estate and took to a wandering life – probably after the death of John Dalton's wife, which took place when he was about twenty-six. He discovered that the world outside was a prayerless place indeed and he determined to do his best to change it for the better. In his young (and, sad to say, later no longer young) arrogance, he criticised everybody, from the King to the Pope; and his contempt for the clergy was profound, especially for their attitude to women:

"Putting the eternal behind them, they seek to flourish in bodily comfort and love. They sin grievously, and do so most in that they have taken holy orders and then go to women as wooers, saying that they languish for their love, and are nearly fainting with great desire and strife of thought; and in this way they deceive women and lead them, light and unstable, to wretchedness."

But what really made him burn was the narrowness of the priesthood: "They forbid excellent men to preach and allow others to do so who have no mission from God; they reject the hermits . . . woe to the priests who with such zeal and clamour exact tithes and payments for sacraments."

Naturally his worst enemies were those very priests whom he detested. Comper tells us that "they ridiculed him as a saint without miracles; found fault with his idle inactivity, his contemplation without works, his independence without obedience. They despised him as a layman and questioned his learning. . . . 'They said he could not preach, and despised his words because he was poor and had no reputation among the great. His teaching is to them a mystery, and they say he errs in his interpretation of Holy Scripture.' Even thus early he was rejected because he was classed as a modernist. He was an innovator and an upstart."

In hitting back, Rolle even went so far as to include his bishop. "Behold a youth," he wrote, "animated with righteous zeal, rises up against an elder, *a hermit against a bishop*; and against *all*, however great, who say that the height of sanctity consists in outward acts. . . . Man is not holier or higher for the outward works that he does. Truly God that is the Beholder of the heart rewards the will more than the deed. The deeds truly hang on the will, not the will on the deeds."

It is likely that at the beginning of his teaching life Rolle was forbidden to preach, but later he became far less outraged at such obstacles because he learnt that love conquers pain. He was helped by the friendship (almost entirely in letters) of an enclosed anchoress, Margaret Kirkby, for whom he wrote a short book, *The Form of Living*. Indeed nuns were always attracted to him and he wrote many sermons for them. It was in a cell attached to a convent at Hampole in south Yorkshire that he spent the last years of his life and, as with other mystics in this book, they were undoubtedly his best. He said:

"It is good to be a preacher; to exert oneself, to go hither and thither, and to be weary for the salvation of souls; but it is better, safer and sweeter by far to pass one's life in contemplation, to feel the nearness of eternal sweetness, to sing the joys of eternal love, and to be rapt in the praise of the Creator by the pouring forth of heavenly songs." It is said that he was often so absorbed when he prayed that once when his cloak in which he was covered was taken from him, he did not feel it; and when, after patching and stitching it, they replaced it on him he did not notice it.

At one time he did try to bring together other like-minded hermits so that they could live as a community, but apparently the venture did not succeed.

"Alas, miserable that I am, so lonely am I that I thus can find no one in my day who desires to come with me and sitting and in silence will yearn after the joys of eternal love."

He died at the age of forty-nine, almost certainly of the Black Death which at that time was ravaging Yorkshire. A local farmer was moved to build him a tomb and there were many recorded miracles of healing for those who visited it, so without doubt he ended his life as a revered holy man. It is interesting to see what constituted a miracle in those days. When the farmer brought the stones to build the tomb it is recorded, "One day, therefore, while he was occupied with the aforesaid work of piety, and had got ready twelve oxen for the drawing, it happened that when he reached the gate of the churchyard at Hampole carrying great stones, his poor beasts by an unhappy accident turned aside from the path, and the cart collided with the side-port of the gate and cast the said stones with great force upon Roger himself. Yet he was in no wise hurt by this, nor felt any shaking or pain of body; and though his foot was tightly jammed by the stones, he was able to get it out without injury to foot or leg. And, indeed, that this miracle should not be forgotten, one of these stones was set up at the gate of the churchyard, so that those coming in might see it; and another is placed on the tomb of the saint."

Rolle's form of mysticism was an outflowing one. Unlike Eckhart, he did not think in terms of God within, or of 'being' God, or the 'isness' which is the core of Eckhart's greatness; but far more of the soul on a journey outwards, fleeing the body and joining its Lover.

"Love truly will not suffer a loving soul to remain in itself, but ravishes it out to the Lover, that the soul is more there where it loves, than where the body is that lives and feels it. . . . What is it truly to feel joy but to have the goodness we need; of it to think, and in it to rest? No marvel that mirth is sweet when true lovers accord, and where the merry solace is of the touching of love; truly the desire of burning lovers is unable to be told, and the sight and speech of each to the other is sweet to them above honey and the honey-comb."

Thus Rolle's teaching was less concerned with seeing into the self than with persuading men and women to a similar state of adoration to his own. He knew that the 'heavenly song' of highest contemplation was a special grace given to him particularly and never hesitated to say so; yet he also believed that the divine melody could be heard by anyone who abandoned themselves in his way to love of the 'Maker'. So his teaching was mainly exhortation, begging men to repent their forgetfulness of God, and their self-centred lives; to give up wealth and luxury and live simply; to pray and meditate constantly in order to find their true Love and Centre of their lives. He thought of the fire of love, which was not only the title of one of his books but also the whole theme of his life, as a refining fire which must sear the soul with heat and flame until, purified by purgation, it is brought to Christ.

"From the great fire of love such a great beauty of virtue grows in souls that a good man would rather choose to suffer all pain than once grieve God."

To 'choose to suffer all pain', or, indeed, to suffer any pain, may seem a distortion of religion to our modern materialistic minds. And yet to some of us it would be intolerable pain to gain all the comfort in the world but never, say, to hear good music again – or to have society so mechanised that there would be no more need to work, but in the process to lose all our woods and fields. Let us do without the bodily comfort, we may say, so long as we can keep the beauty. And in the same way, the person who feels the numinous clarity of all things in a moment of wonder would undoubtedly rather choose to suffer some worldly deprivation than to be denied the possibility of that experience again.

"While the soul gathers all the self into endless mirth of loving," says Rolle, "she withholds herself inwardly and does not flow out to seek bodily delights. And because she is fed inwardly with inner happiness, it is not surprising that she may long for You, and seeing You face to face, be joined to You without end."

Rolle tried hard and constantly to make the point that the contemplative life is a *happy* one. To the uninitiated it seems that life without worldly pleasures must be barren in the extreme – or at least that a life centred on mystery could not compensate for the loss of the world. In fact it is this particular point which holds most people back from even testing the water, let alone taking the plunge. Yet a mainly contemplative life holds a quality of joy and a level of happiness which simply cannot be found in any man-made occupation. Hinduism has recognised this fact from its remote beginnings and one of its great teachings – one which Rolle would surely have endorsed – is that there are four stages to man's spiritual life, each leading on to a higher state of joy. The first is pleasure of body and mind in all the good things of life – a fairly simple level of enjoyment which is necessarily limited by the goods available. When that ceases to satisfy, man's next desire is usually for prestige, status, power and wealth – in other words for worldly success. When this is seen to be time-bound and ephemeral he moves on to a more selfless pleasure – that of helping mankind and putting the claims of others before his own. He has started to want to give rather than to get. Finally this too seems inadequate as a goal and although he may still continue the work, his final fulfilment seems to lead beyond the community to another dimension altogether – to a more timeless happiness based on a new realisation of his inner life.

Rolle saw such an ascension as the turning towards an ever deeper and greater love.

"Three degrees of love I shall tell you, for I want that you might win to the highest. The first degree is called Insuperable; the second Inseparable; and the third is Singular.

"Your love is insuperable when it is not overcome by selfishness but is stalwart against all temptations; and then it is balanced and stable whether you are in ease or in anguish, in health or in sickness; so that men see that you would not, even if you were given the whole world, make God angry at any time; and that you would rather suffer all the pain and woe that might come to any creature before you would displease Him. In this manner your love will be insuperable – nothing will be able to bring it down, but it will always spring on high. . . .

"Inseparable is your love when all your heart, your thought and your strength is so wholly, so entirely, and so perfectly fastened, set and established in Jesus Christ that your thought never goes from him, never departs from him, sleeping excepted, and as soon as you wake your heart is on him . . . when you can at no time forget him, waking or sleeping, whatever you do or say, then your love is inseparable. . . .

"The third degree is the highest and most wondrous to win. It is called singular for it has no equal. Singular love is when all comfort and solace has left your heart and there is only Jesus Christ alone. It has no delight in any other joy. For the sweetness that is in this degree is his love, so comforting and so lasting; so burning and gladdening, that he or she who is in this degree can feel the fire of love burning in their soul as well as you can feel your finger burn if you put it in the fire. But that fire, if it is hot, is so delectable and so wonderful that I cannot even describe it.

"In the first degree are many people; in the second degree are full few; but in the third degree are scarcely any; for the greater the perfection the fewer followers it has.

"In the first degree men are likened to the stars; in the second to the moon; in the third to the sun. 'Therefore,' says St Paul, 'others of the sun, others of the moon, others of the stars'; so it is with the lovers of God. In this third degree, if you can win your way to it, you shall know more joy than I can ever tell you of."

Rolle spoke constantly of love. He poured on to the image of Christ in his heart all the love of which he was capable. Almost one wearies of the word in his prose for there seems to be a danger of a sort of idolatry. He was not noted for his general love to mankind. Did he build an image in his mind of the Perfect Person whom he could love without measure – even with a repressed sexuality – and then attach the name Jesus to it? This is possible but not really probable – a mental image does not last, or stay the same, any more than a physical one does, and Rolle's Jesus was the means by which he transcended himself in outpourings of love all his life. It went beyond him, it was more than him. In the end we should grant that he had a genuine intuition of the God-ground and that this was the real and proper mainstay of his life – as he expresses it here:

"O sweet and delectable light that is my Maker unmade; enlighten the seeing of my inward eye with clearness unmade, that my mind, speedily cleansed from uncleanness and marvellous with gifts, may swiftly fly into the high mirth of love; and kindled with your savour, I may sit and rest, joying in you, Jesu. And as it were ravished in heavenly sweetness, and made stable in the beholding of things unseen, never elsewhere shall I be gladdened except by godly things.

"O love everlasting, enflame my soul to love God, so that nothing may burn in me but His embraces. O good Jesu, who shall allow me to feel you that now may neither be felt nor seen? Shed yourself into the entrails of my soul. Come into my heart and fill it with your clearest sweetness. Moisten my mind with the hot wine of your sweet love, that I will forget all ills and all scorning and imaginings, and only having you, I may be glad and joy in Jesu, my Lord. Henceforth, sweetest God, do not go from me, continually bide with me in your sweetness; for your presence alone is solace to me, and your absence alone leaves me heavy.

"O Holy Ghost that gives grace where you will, come into me and ravish me to you; change the nature that you have made with honeyed gifts, so that my soul, fulfilled with your loving joy, may despise and cast away all the things of this world.

Ghostly gifts my soul may take of you, the Giver, and going by songful joy into indescribable light may she all be melted in holy love. Burn my reins and my heart with fire that on your altar I may endlessly burn."

Meister Eckhart

"Up then, noble soul! Put on your jumping shoes which are intellect and love, and overleap the worship of your mental powers, overleap your understanding and spring into the heart of God, into his hiddenness where you are hidden from all creatures."

It is impossible to touch the surface of medieval mysticism without at once coming into contact with Eckhart. In his strong yet gentle personality, and tough yet flexible intellect, were brought harmoniously together all the strands and influences of the preceding centuries, to be recognised and realised anew. His influence on the mystics of his own generation and of succeeding ones was very great; in fact, as Evelyn Underhill points out, the German and Flemish mystics of the thirteenth and fourteenth centuries all differed greatly in temperament and teaching yet all held something in common – something which was shared by no other school – and that something came from Eckhart, for all were in touch with his teaching either directly or as friends and pupils of his disciples.

He stands in equal rank to his own great teachers, Augustine, Dionysius, Erigena, and Albertus Magnus. Equal and perhaps higher, for few of them were able to become, in like bold simplicity, the interpreter of the mystery of the God-ground to the common people in their own tongue, for he taught both in Latin and in his own German dialect.

His great energy and zeal in teaching, and above all his powerful and creative mind, brought about two things. The first was condemnation by the Church for heresy, for pushing his understanding 'beyond the flaming bounds of time and space'; and the second a recent but far-reaching and over-whelming appreciation of him during the last century and this, so that he is now ranked as one of the great teachers of all time. Rudolf Otto has compared him to Shankara, the Vedantist philosopher of the eleventh century; Dr Suzuki believed him to be the equal of the Zen patriarchs; the philosopher Hegel took him as a teacher, as did Martin Heidegger.

Little is known about his personal life, although some information has gradually come to light. He was born, probably to a noble family, in or near Hochheim in Thuringia, close to the year 1260. When he was about fifteen he entered a Dominican priory at Erfurt, near his home. The course of studies for a Dominican priest was nine years long, and although he began at Erfurt his unusual capabilities were soon recognised and for the next step in his education he was sent to the famous Dominican Higher School in Cologne, where he was probaby just in time to hear Albert the Great – the only scholar of the Middle Ages to be given the title Magnus, and the teacher of Thomas Aquinas – who died in 1280.

In 1302 Eckhart – no longer a young man – was in Paris, having been selected to study at the eminent school of theology there. This was a great honour and was prompted perhaps by the fact that he was already Prior of Erfurt and Vicar of Thuringia. His earliest German work, *The Talks of Instruction*, was written before he went to Paris and may well have influenced his superiors in sending him to earn yet higher honours. At any rate, after some time in Paris he received the title of Meister (Master) of Theology and was henceforth always known as Meister Eckhart. But he was not very impressed by his new role nor by the life of scholarship which he had observed. There are some passages which sum up his feelings about the life of theological scholars. In one he says: "There are many masters among us who have used the Bible for thirty years or more and who understand it now in its unity as little as a cow or horse would."

When he left Paris he was chosen to be the first Provincial-Prior of the Dominican Order for Saxony, which meant a territory covering most of north Germany and Holland; and in 1307 he was given the extra task of being Vicar-General of Bohemia, a province notorious for lax discipline and 'heretical' views in its convents. As he was supposed to lead all these erring monks and nuns to a more Church-oriented way of life, he himself must have been considered quite free from unorthodoxy although ironically, as M. Walshe has pointed out, it was at just about that time that he wrote *The Book of Divine Comfort* for the recently widowed Queen Agnes of Hungary – a work which later was to be quoted against him in his trial for heresy.

For some time conflict and sharp disagreement had been growing between the Dominicans and the Franciscans. Eckhart's opponent in debate in Paris had been the Spanish Gonsalvus, who later became General of the Franciscans, and in 1311 Eckhart was recalled to Paris – ostensibly for more study but more probably in order to defend the Dominican scholars against the Franciscans. It is not known how long he stayed, nor what effect he had, but in 1314 he was in Strasbourg, where he properly began his great career as a preacher.

At that time the city of Strasbourg was the renowned religious centre of Germany. Scholars and heretics, monks and nuns and Beghards, all were to be found there. It was a rule of the Dominican Order that the spiritual training of nuns should be undertaken by 'highly learned brothers' and it is certain that Eckhart himself was one of those who were deeply concerned with the nuns in the seven convents of the city. One nun of the period is reported to have written: "Wise Meister Eckhart speaks to us about Nothingness. He who does not understand that, in him the Divine light has never shone."

At this time the Beghards and Beguines (see Introduction) were numerous in Strasbourg and were already under suspicion by the Church. It would be interesting to know what Eckhart felt about such free-thinkers but unfortunately nothing positive has emerged, although Karl Schmidt has tried to show that Eckhart was in sympathy with the Beghards and knew them well – for, as Walshe points out, they were often less 'heretical' than simply trying to help themselves, while the Church floundered in a morass of brutish suppressions and struggles for power.

Whatever his sympathies, it was here in Strasbourg and later in Cologne that Eckhart developed a reputation which has reverberated down the centuries for profound and beautifully worded sermons which cut like a diamond to the core of truth.

One thing he always maintained (and it was the basis later on of his defence against the charge of heresy); he considered himself to be as much in harmony with the teachings of the Church as Thomas Aquinas had been. He did not want to take anything away from essential Christianity, any more than he wanted to add anything – but he did want to express it anew, *as he saw it*. He wanted to give abundant life to those truths which he thought were ignored or misunderstood, but it never occurred to him to substitute new content for old. The Christian message was his message and its life was his life. But he wanted to show people other ways of looking at this message than had, say, Thomas Aquinas.

These – his other ways of looking – are home to some of us and foreign ground to others. For instance when Eckhart wanted to impress upon his hearers the need for imageless contemplation he used Christ's words: 'It is expedient for you that I go away: for if I do not go away the Holy Spirit will not come unto you.' And he explained these words by saying: "It is as if he said: You have taken too much joy in *my present image*, therefore the perfect joy of the Holy Spirit cannot be in you."

Alan Watts once said: "we are spiritually paralysed by the fetish of Jesus. . . . His literary image in the Gospels has, through centuries of homage, become far more of an idol than anything graven in wood or stone, so that today the most genuinely reverent act of worship is to destroy that image."

Eckhart would not perhaps have said destroy, but go beyond. Perfect disinterest, or non-attachment, was the phrase he often used. "Discard the form," he begged, "and be joined to the formless essence, for the spiritual comfort of God is very subtle and is not extended except to those who can leave behind physical comfort."

Physical comfort for the pious might include images of Christ and Mary, the words of the mass and prayers, candles lit to the Virgin, the beads of the rosary. And even for the undevotional there were comforts such as quietness and solitude, beauty of created things and of natural objects, to which we all cling. Such advice as Eckhart gave would not, one would have thought, have made him popular, and yet he became the most well-known and loved preacher in Germany. Why? Is there perhaps a true longing in the human heart, both then and now, for release from our attachment to created things, however finely spiritual they may seem to be?

If so, then Eckhart was determined to bring it out into the open. "He who seeks God under settled form lays hold of the form, while missing the God concealed in it. . . . Thus we say that a person should be so poor [empty] that he is not, and has no place for God to act in. To reserve a place would be to maintain distinctions. Therefore I pray God that *he may rid me of God*, for my essential being is above God in so far as we comprehend God as the principle of creatures."

The way in which Eckhart understood existence was through the relationship between the Godhead (or God-ground) and God. The first was to him utter beingness itself, the 'isness' of all things; whereas the second was creation, the 'becoming' of all things.

"God and the Godhead are as different from each other as heaven and earth. . . . God *becomes* where all creatures express him: there he becomes 'God'. When I existed in the core, the soil, the river, the source of the Godhead, no one asked me where I was going or what I was doing. There was no one there to ask me, but the moment I emerged, the world of creatures began to shout: 'God!' If someone were to ask me: 'Brother Eckhart, when did you leave home?' – that would indicate that I must have been at home sometime. I was there just now, in fact. It is in this way that creatures speak of God – but why do they not mention the godhead? Because there is only unity in the godhead and there is nothing to talk about. God acts. The godhead does not. It has nothing to do and there is nothing going on in it. It never is on the lookout for something to do. The difference between God and the godhead is the difference between action and nonaction. . . . The godhead gave all things up to God. The godhead is poor, naked and empty as though it were not; it has not, wills not, wants not, gets not. It is God who has the treasure and the bride in him, the godhead is as void as though it were not."

How reminiscent this is of the *Tao Te Ching*:

> The unnamed is heaven and earth's origin;
> Naming is the mother of ten thousand things.
> Whenever there is no desire one beholds the
>   mystery;

Whenever there is desire one beholds the
  manifestations.
When people lost sight of the way to live
Came codes of love and honesty.

When people lost sight of the godhead, they shouted 'God!'
is what Eckhart is implying. He continues: "When I come into
the core, the soil, the stream, and the source of the godhead, no
one asks me where I'm coming from or where I've been. No one
has missed me in the place where 'God' ceases to become."

Such an amazing statement – that there is a Ground where
'God' ceases to become! It is no wonder he finished his sermon
by saying: "If anyone has understood this sermon, I wish him
well. If no one had been here, I would have had to preach it
to this offering box. There are some poor [baffled] people who
will return to their homes and say: 'I shall sit down, eat my loaf
of bread, and serve God.' I swear, however, that these people
will have to remain in their errors, for they can never attain
what these others attain who follow God in poverty and exile."

Yet Eckhart's understanding of God as Creator and the
godhead as beyond creation, goes to the very heart of religious
knowledge. And he expresses most vividly how we experience
the two within us:

"To my outer man, creatures taste like creatures, as do wine,
bread and meat. To my inner man, however, they taste like
gifts of God rather than creatures, and to my inmost being they
are not even like gifts of God, but rather are timeless."

To interpret this is perhaps to put it thus: in our ordinary
life we use our five senses as gateways through which an
unending stream of impressions pours in – which are instantly
and unknowingly by us translated by our nervous system, and
the appropriate response given. For instance, the colour of a
flower gives rise to a process in my eye and brain through which
I perceive the colour. But this sensory process does not show
me things in their deepest sense, only in their physical
appearance. The next thing that happens – and this too is
virtually an unconscious process – is that the input presented
by my nervous system (which would be quite a different input
if I were a cat or a bird) is pounced on by my brain and sorted,
categorised and classified, some parts accepted, some rejected,

until a 'concept' or symbol is arrived at which represents the initial sense-impression. I then look upon this concept *as* the object it represents and believe this to be the external world with, as Underhill puts it, 'enviable and amazing simplicity, attributing our own sensations to the unknown world'. The flower *is* red, the sea *is* blue. It is very hard to accept that these 'facts' are only impressions and ideas, but it needs but a slight investigation to show that our concepts cannot be relied on to represent reality (the classic instance being of a number of people all witnessing the same event but whose accounts all differ).

"Every time the powers of the soul come into contact with created things," says Eckhart, "they receive the *created* images and likenesses from the created thing and absorb them. In this way arises the soul's knowledge of created things. Created things cannot come nearer to the soul than this, and the soul can only approach created things by the voluntary reception of images. And it is through the presence of the image that the soul approaches the created world: for *the image is a thing which the soul creates* with her own powers. Does the soul want to know the nature of a stone – a horse – a man? She forms an image."

We would not be human did we not conceptualise – it is what our humanity and certainly our civilisation is based on. But the danger lies in over-conceptualisation, when we not only symbolise every object but ourselves as well. When this happens I lose my reality because my concept shows me to be one object among other objects; my eye and the colour of the flower seem to be two different entities, as does my being and the flower's being. This is to taste man as man and bread as bread – this is Eckhart's outer man.

But the colour and the flower, together with my eye and brain, are really one unified field of action, one inseparable reality, forever in motion. As Capra points out: "Particles are not things but interconnections between things; and these things are interconnections between other things, and so on. Thus quantum theory reveals the basic oneness of the universe . . . things and phenomena are perceived as being different manifestations of the same reality. The division of the world into separate objects, though useful and practical on the everyday level, is seen as an illusion . . . quantum theory forces us to see the universe not as a collection of physical objects, but rather as a complicated web of relations between the various parts of a unified whole."

This leads us to Eckhart's second way of seeing things – of 'tasting everything as gifts of God' – as parts of a unified whole. It is perhaps easier to grasp this intellectually than to live it and to have direct experience of it. For to live it is to let go the feeling of separation between object and self.

Let us assume for one minute that you have no head. You are headless. At this moment whatever you are looking at has replaced your head. If you actually *do* this, the sensation of being a separate entity vanishes and is replaced by a non-duality which Thomas Merton calls Absolute Seeing. "There is just seeing. Seeing what? Not an Absolute Object but Absolute Seeing."

This is clearly expressed in Buddhism. When we practise 'bare attention' we just see what is there without adding any comment, interpretation, judgement or conclusion. There is just attending. Learning to see in this way is the basic practice of Buddhist meditation. The self does not come into it. 'To forget the self is to be enlightened by all things' said Dogen. We forget the self when we are headless in this way of seeing, and then every object appears indeed to 'taste like a gift of God'. For when we observe that the world is not ours, that even the chair on which I sit and the paper spread out before me are, in their essence, *unknowable* by me, then we can become aware of the supreme and total mystery of existence, which is reality. When I take away from an object all my projected ideas of it, and my feelings about it, I am then able to see it *not* as a mere object of experience and use, but as itself, supremely real in its own right, clearly shining in its own light.

'Tasting everything as gifts of God' is indeed a way of seeing and being which can only be described by inadequate words, such as joy and delight. In that taste all things are experienced in their 'isness'. "I am sure", says Eckhart, "that if a soul knew the very least of all that being means, it would never turn away from it."

"The soul is troubled so long as it perceives created things in their separateness" he says. "All that is created, or all that is capable of being created, is nothing. But so long as the soul beholds forms, even though she sees an angel, or herself as something formed – so long there is imperfection in her. Yes, indeed, should she even behold God [as separate], in so far as He is with form and number in the Trinity – so long there is imperfection in her. But when you taste God . . . all things become to you pure God, because in all things you see nothing but pure God. Like one who looks long into the sun – what he afterwards may see is seen full of the sun.''

It must be pointed out, however, that this experience excludes imagination. We are very inclined, when we are in the 'outer man' state of feeling isolated and separate within our bodies, to attribute to other people and things the sort of emotions that we ourselves feel. This is not true emptiness, according to Eckhart. Instead it is what Steiner calls an 'anthropomorphising world view'. He says: "When he confronts us externally, we perceive only sensory features in another man. I cannot look into the interior of my fellow man. From what I see and hear of him I make inferences as to his interior, his soul. Thus the soul is never something I perceive directly. I can perceive a soul only within myself. No man can see my thoughts, my imaginings, my feelings. And just as *I* have an inner life besides the one which can be perceived externally, so [I think] that all other beings have one too – this is the conclusion of one who takes the position of the anthropomorphising world view. That part of a plant which I perceive externally must in the same way [or so I believe] be only the outside of an interior, of a soul, which in my thoughts I must add to what I actually perceive. And since there exists for me only a single inner world, namely my own, I can only imagine the inner world of other beings to be similar to my own. Thus one reaches a sort of universal animation of all nature (panpsychism).'' He adds: "But my personal inner life, my thoughts, memories and feelings, are in me because I am a creature of nature with such and such an organisation, with a sensory apparatus, with a certain nervous system. . . . When I transfer this interior to external things [people or objects] I am in fact indulging in idle fancy.''

And indeed such 'idle fancy' comes between us and the true reality – the 'isness' of a thing. It is specifically what Eckhart and others ask us to drop. We are to awaken ourselves to a higher apprehension than mere imagination and fantasy. What we must awaken to is Absolute Seeing, in which a human, animal or plant appears to us directly, *as it is in itself*. There is no need for me to endow a flower with anything of mine – it is as it is, and in its 'isness' I can rejoice.

On casual reading, it might appear that to stop imagining the thoughts and feelings of others is cold and heartless; and that it is *because* of our imagination that we can reach below the surface into another's state of mind and sympathetically perhaps alleviate his suffering. This belief is absolutely true, but it is because we are *awakening to reality* that we become more sensitive to the evidence placed before us. All our senses become more attuned to the world of reality, to the *facts*, indeed to the haven of 'God's gifts' in which we live and act. Then when we see suffering we are able to help because of our life of reality and not because we are imagining what the sufferer is feeling, or endowing him with a whole range of emotions he may not have. We help because the evidence which our real seeing of him brings prompts a real action – or even perhaps no action at all.

But what of Eckhart's third, inmost being, where creatures are not even creatures and even God is left behind – 'they are not like the gifts of God but are timeless'? Only he can expand on this.

"From time to time I tell of the one power in the soul which alone is free. Sometimes I have called it the tabernacle of the soul; sometimes a spiritual light, anon I say it is a spark. But now I say: it is neither this nor that. Yet it is somewhat: somewhat more exalted over this and that than the heavens are above the earth. . . . It is of all names free, of all forms void: exempt and free as God is in himself."

He adds: "There is something, transcending the soul's created nature, not accessible to creatures, non-existent as we term existence; no angel has it, for his is a clear nature, and clear and defined things have no concern with this. It is akin to God, intrinsically one, having nothing in common with nothing. Many a priest finds it a baffling thing. It is one; rather unnamed than named, rather unknown than known. If you could naught yourself in an instant, less than an instant, I should say, all that this is in itself would belong to you. But while you have any mind for yourself at all you know no more of God than my mouth does of colour or my eye of taste: so little you know, you discern, what God is."

"Bohm asserts", says Gary Zukav, putting this statement into the words of a scientist, "that the most fundamental level is an unbroken wholeness which is, in his words, 'that-which-is'. All things, including space, time and matter, are forms of that-which-is. There is an order which is enfolded into the very process of the universe, but that enfolded order may not be readily apparent."

Our 'inmost being', then, is part of the godhead, which is beyond all definition. "The ground of the mind and the ground of God are one sole essential being" said Eckhart.

"Therefore, I say that to the extent a person can deny himself and turn away from created things, he will find his unity and blessing in that little spark in the soul, which neither space nor time touches. The spark is averse to creatures, and favourable only to pure God as he is in himself. It is not satisfied with the Father, nor the Son, nor the Holy Spirit, nor with all three persons together, as long as their individual properties are preserved. To tell the truth, this light is not satisfied with the unity either, of this fruitful conception of the divine nature, but I shall go further and say what must sound strange – though I am really speaking the truth – that this light is not satisfied by the simple, still, motionless essence of the divine being that neither gives nor takes. It is more interested in knowing where this essence came from. It wants to penetrate the simple core, the still desert, into which no distinction ever crept – neither the Father, the Son, nor the Holy Spirit. It wants to get into the secret, to which no man is privy, where it is satisfied by a Light whose unity is greater than its own. This core is a simple stillness, which is unmoved itself but by whose immobility all things are moved and all receive life, that is to say, all people who live by reason and have their centre within themselves."

It seems to be almost the godhead of godheads that Eckhart is talking of. Certainly he means that we should go beyond creation and the creator to that which is the source of all – the uncreated, unconditioned and time-free. For this is our 'inmost being' and when we reach that inmost base of ourselves then all the world of phenomena, all creatures, are seen as equal in existence, distinct but not different.

"All that a man has here externally in multiplicity is intrinsically One. Here all blades of grass, wood, and stone, all things are One. This is the deepest depth."

And again, Eckhart insists: "If the soul knows God in creatures, night falls. If it sees how they have their being in God, morning breaks. But if it sees the Being that is in God himself alone, it is high noon! See! This is what one ought to desire with mad fervour – that all his life should become Being.

"But we are so dead that neither good nor evil affect us. Thus, what we know we must know to its roots, for we shall never know anything until we know its causes. There can be no knowledge until knowing reaches the hidden reasons. Thus, too, life cannot be perfected until it has returned to its secret source, where life is Being, a life this soul receives when it dies even down to its roots, so that we may live that life yonder which itself is Being. One scholar points out what it is that hinders us from that: we are hindered by cleaving to time. Whatever clings to time is mortal. . . . The whole scattered world of lower things is gathered up to oneness when the soul climbs up to that life in which there are no opposites. Entering this life . . . opposites are forgotten, but where this light does not fall, things fall away to death and destruction."

Here we come to the crux of Eckhart's understanding – that we must identify ourselves 'to the roots' with our inmost being: "Scripture says that we have to become like God (John 3:2). 'Like' – the word is bad and deceptive. If I liken myself to someone else, and if I find someone who is like me, then this man behaves as if he were I, although he is not, and deceives people about it. Many things look like gold, but since they are not, they lie. In the same way all things pretend to be 'like' God; but they are lying since they are not like him. God can no more suffer likeness than he can suffer not being God. Likeness is something that does not occur in God; what does occur in the Godhead and in eternity is oneness. But likeness is not oneness. Whenever I am one with someone I am not like him. There is nothing alien in oneness. In eternity there is only oneness but not likeness."

143

Likeness, then, is created and is in opposition to unlikeness. But there can be no opposition in oneness because it transcends all opposites. Eckhart used the analogy of fire to explain his point: "Fire transforms all things it touches into its own nature. The wood does not change the fire into itself, but the fire changes the wood into itself. In the same way we are transformed into God so that we may know him as he is. Acting and becoming are one. God and I are one in this work; he acts and I become." And he adds: "God is not found in distinction. When the mind reaches the original image and finds itself alone in it, then it finds God. Finding itself and finding God is one single process, outside of time. As far as it penetrates into him, it is identical with God . . . not included, nor united, but more: identical."

Eckhart believed that we long to be identical with God and are not fulfilled until we are. In this world we seek for this state constantly, and some of us are lucky enough to find a reflection of it in music or art or nature – when the actor and the action become one. In the West we have no word for such an experience, but the Chinese use the word *li*, meaning innermost reality. *Li* transcends form and yet it is inherent in every atom. Any painter, for instance, should identify himself with the *li* (or suchness) of what he paints, so that the painting will reveal the *li* of the subject. He must do this by sacrificing his own ego, for the perception of *li* can only occur when the feeling of me, my and mine is out of the way. A painting which is not based on the intuitive apprehension of the *li* of its subject is not considered worthy of true art, no matter how carefully and faithfully the painting might reflect external shapes and colours.

"Let us learn self-forgetting until we call nothing more our own" said Eckhart.

He saw various ways in which creation identifies itself in us and in which we identify ourselves through creation. Building a family or a community, for instance; or in an exchange of thoughts in which 'two words of existence' are actualised; or in co-operating with life itself to such an extent that we are at one with whatever occurs – which means living right *in* the situations which are the reality of the life we are now encountering. This is particularly hard for westerners, who usually prefer to alter external circumstances rather than to go into them. But if, for instance, we run to catch a bus and it goes off without us, our inner feeling can still be at one with the circumstance, accepting that the time of waiting for the next bus has its own new and particular reality. Then we shall be in harmony with that interval, instead of regarding it simply as the object of our impatience. If it is merely a wasted time, to be got through somehow, we will have lost our identity with it and have separated ourselves from it and from the chance of becoming one with the scenery of our lives.

"We ought to learn", says Eckhart, "how to keep a free mind in all we do, but it is rare that an untrained person can do this in such a way that neither circumstance nor jobs bother him. Expert attention is necessary. To be aware of God at all times and to be enlightened by him under all circumstances equally, there are two special requirements. First: to be spiritually quite private, guarding the mind carefully against irrelevant ideas, so as to keep them out and not deal with them, giving them no place in your life. The second has to do with the mind's own intentions, whether spontaneous in the mind or representing some object, or whatever their nature. Do not be dissipated in such ideas lest you become lost in the crowd of them. . . .

"You may say: But when a person has a job to do, he must give his attention to it and thus has to concentrate on external things, for it takes an idea to make a job possible. And that is quite true, but the connection of ideas to things is, for the good man, simply a means of bringing about the divine and spiritual.

"People ought not to consider so much what they are to do as what they *are*; let them but *be* good and their ways and deeds will shine brightly. If you are just, your actions will be just too. Do not think that saintliness comes from occupation; it depends rather on what one is. The kind of work we do does not make us holy but we may make it holy. However 'sacred' a calling may be, as it is a calling, it has no power to sanctify; but rather as we *are* and have the divine ground within, we bless each task we do, be it eating, or sleeping, or watching, or any other. Whatever they do who have not much of [God's] nature, they work in vain.

"Thus take care that your emphasis is laid on *being* good and not on the number or kind of things to be done. Emphasise rather the fundamentals on which your work depends."

Everyday practice, then, is the greatest aid to the actual experience of egolessness and of an undifferentiated life. Because as long as we still continue to hold to one thing as better for us than another, we are bound to suffer. "As long as any difference belonging to created things gets response in the mind, it thereby feels chagrin", said Eckhart.

In fact, for him, non-attachment to one's own interests was the greatest virtue. He says he sought earnestly for "the best and highest virtue where a man may knit himself most narrowly to God . . . and wherein was no difference between himself and God, before God created creature". He finds it in true lack of attachment to all created things.

"True detachment means a mind as little moved by what befalls, by joy and sorrow, honour and disgrace, as a broad mountain by a gentle breeze. Such motionless detachment makes a man superlatively God-like. For that God is God is due to his motionless detachment, and it is from his detachment that he gets his purity and his simplicity and immutability. If then a man is going to be as God . . . it will be by detachment. This leads to purity and from purity to simplicity and from simplicity to immovability; and it is these three which constitute the identity between man and God, which identity is grace, for it is grace which draws a man away from mortal things and purges him of time. I would have you know that to be empty of creatures is to be full of God and to be full of creatures is to be empty of God.

"Someone may object, but was Christ in motionless detachment when he cried: 'My soul is sorrowful even unto death'? Or Mary, when she stood beneath his cross? For much is said about her lamentations. How is all this compatible with motionless detachment?" In other words, how are our natural grief and joy compatible with immovableness? Here Eckhart brings forth his understanding of man as twofold – an understanding which is echoed by other mystics.

"Know then, that according to philosophers there are in every man two men; one, the outward man, is his objective nature: this man is served by the five senses, and he is energised by the power of the soul. The other man, the inner man, is man's subjective nature."

The outward man, then, is our ordinary, everyday, conditioned organism, reacting to stimuli from the five senses, which are themselves wholly dependent for their input on the environment around them; so in this sense we are objectified – indeed, at this level we are not only a continuous connection between one part of the world and another, as modern physics tells us, but we also cannot be separated from our *function*, which is to be human:

"Quantum theory has shown that particles are not isolated grains of matter, but are probability patterns, interconnections in an inseparable cosmic web. Relativity theory, so to speak, has made these patterns come alive by revealing their intrinsically dynamic character. It has shown that the activity of matter is the very essence of its being. The particles of the subatomic world are not only active in the sense of moving around very fast; they themselves are *processes*! The existence of matter and its activity cannot be separated. They are but different aspects of the same space-time reality." (Capra, *The Tao of Physics*.)

When Eckhart refers to man as being 'energised by the power of the soul', he means that the God-ground is the energising factor in *all* life, down to the minutest sub-particle, and is known to us by means of our soul – what one could describe as that part of us which is original, individual, unlike any other creature. (The term 'soul' is a sticky one to define since Eastern religions do not have it and Christianity is often a bit uncertain itself. In Eckhart's eyes, however, it seems to be the mind – not the physical brain – but the 'mind' which is our individual self; the bridge between our animal existence dictated by the five senses and that particular sense of self which distinguishes us from all other creatures.)

"The other man," Eckhart continues, "the inner man, is man's subjective nature." In Eckhart's eyes, *not* subjective in a psychological sense, for all that belongs to the outer man – but subjective because it is the part of ourselves that we cannot define or objectify. It is the essential innerness, which cannot itself be described – or it would not be truly inner – but which can best be related to 'I' rather than to 'me'. 'Me' belongs to 'my' and 'mine' and is entirely objectified. But the word 'I' has a limitless connotation – 'I am that I am' – the 'I amness' of ourselves is infinite. Indeed, as St Bernard pointed out, it is by reflecting on who and what we truly are – on that very 'I amness' – that we begin to apprehend what it really is.

"I have been thinking for some time that the fact that *I am a person* is something others hold in common with myself. That I see and hear and eat and drink – this I have in common with other animals, but the fact that *I am* pertains only to me and not to other men or angels, nor even to God, except as I am one with him" says Eckhart. He goes on to say:

"Now I want you to know that the Godly-minded man uses his soul-powers in his outward man no more than his five senses really need it; and his inner man has recourse to the five senses only so far as it is guide and keeper to these five senses. . . ."

The inner man has recourse to the five senses only so far as it is guide and keeper to them – here we come to a very important step on the way. This step, according to Eckhart, is to live in 'I amness' and from that state to direct one's outer life with real non-attachment. Such a way of life means being fully mindful, paying full attention, but never clinging or lingering. The man who lives from his innerness is one whose actions spring spontaneously from a state of receptive emptiness. To reach that state we must give to our senses only what they need and no more. A modern Zen master, Seung Sahn, says: 'don't make anything', by which he means 'don't put into the situation that which isn't there'. Indeed our mind, or 'soul-power', is perfectly able to deal with all situations if we allow it to do its work freely and do not try to add to the situation with imagination or possess it through thought, thus turning it into something different altogether. What Seung Sahn calls a 'don't-know mind' is the clear mind which does not hang on to anything in the way of ideas or preconceptions, and is thus unbounded and free to respond wholly to every situation. This does not mean that one should never *think* – thinking is natural to the human brain and its best tool, but there should be no attachment to the thoughts. Seung Sahn compared the mind to an electronic calculator. As long as the mind is allowed to stay at zero, or as don't-know-mind in its straightforward state, it is like the calculator, ready and clear to deal with whatever programme is put into it. But when a mind already thinks it knows everything, it is like a calculator which has not been cleared of its old programme before a new programme is put in, and so it cannot give the correct answer to the present situation. In this way, having recourse to the five senses only so far as it is guide and keeper to them means keeping the mind at zero, open and clear.

"That man is free who clings to nothing and to whom nothing clings" said Eckhart.

He continues: "What surplus energy she has beyond what she expends on her five senses the soul bestows upon her inner man, and supposing he leans towards some right high endeavour she will call in all the powers she has lent to the five senses and then the man is said to be senseless and rapt away, his object being either some unknowable form or some formless knowable. Remember, God asks every spiritual man to love him with all the power of his soul. 'You shall love the Lord thy God with all your heart', he says. Some squander all their soul-powers on their outward man; namely, those whose thoughts and feelings all hinge on temporal goods, unwitting of an inner man. And even as the awakened man will now and then deprive his outward self of all the powers of the soul when he is embarking on some high adventure, so bestial man will rob his inner self of all its soul-powers to expend them on his outer man. Withal it must be realised that the outward man is able to be active and leave the inward man *entirely passive and unmoved*."

Here we have come to Eckhart's experience of that essence of ourselves which is truly home – the immovable strength which is not swayed by the outer man because it is not dependent on him. 'Settling into the self' is how Buddhism puts it. Eckhart uses the comparison of a door and its hinge: "The door goes to and fro upon its hinges. Now the projecting door I liken to the outward man and the hinge I liken to the inner man. As it shuts and opens the door swings to and fro while the hinge remains unmoved in the same place without undergoing any change. And likewise here."

To find this fundamental hinge we must become – as is

perhaps obvious – 'empty and poor'; and by this Eckhart means true abandonment.

"These days, if someone asks me what a poor person is who wills nothing, I answer and say: 'So long as a person has his own wish in him to fulfil even the ever-beloved will of God, if that is still a matter of his desire then this person does not yet possess the poverty of which we want to speak. Indeed, this person then still has a will with which he or she wants to satisfy God's will, and that is not the right poverty. For if a man wants to be truly poor, he must be as free from his natural will as when he had not yet been born. For truly, as long as you want to do God's will, and yearn for eternity and God, you are not really poor; for he is poor who wills nothing, knows nothing and wants nothing."

In yet stronger terms, a Zen master was once asked by a monk:

"What do you say if I come to you with nothing?"

"Fling it down to the ground!"

Even to hold on to the idea that we can possess nothing is to miss the truth.

"If it is the case", said Eckhart, "that a man is emptied of things, creatures, himself and God, and if still God could find a place in him to act, then we say: as long as that place exists, this man is not poor with the most intimate poverty. For God does not intend that man shall keep a place reserved for *Him* to work in, since true poverty of spirit requires that man shall be emptied of God and of all his works, so that if God wants to act in the soul, he himself must be the place in which he acts. . . .

"'What then shall I do?' You shall lose your you-ness and dissolve in his hisness; your yours shall be his mine, so utterly one mine that you in him shall know timelessly his is-ness, free from becoming: his nameless nothingness."

Perhaps the most unusual aspect of Eckhart's understanding and the one which links him not only with other religions but also with our new discoveries in relativity, is his view of timelessness and its relation to time. The word he frequently uses is *Now* and for him it had immense significance. It is closely linked to his great belief in non-attachment, for this moment Now is free – it is only itself.

In this passage, he links time with emptiness:

"Now mark this word carefully. It must of necessity be a virgin, the person by whom Jesus was received. 'Virgin' is as much as to say a person who is void of alien images, as empty as he was when he did not exist. Now the question may be asked how a man who has been born and has reached the age of rational understanding can be as empty of all images [and ideas] as he was when he was not; for he knows many things, all of which are images; so how can he be empty of them? Note the explanation which I shall give you. If I were possessed of sufficient understanding so as to comprehend within my own mind all the images ever conceived by all men, as well as those that exist in God himself – if I had these without attachment, whether in doing or in leaving undone, without before or after, but rather standing free in this present Now ready to receive God's most beloved will and to do it continually, then in truth I would be a virgin, untrammelled by any images, just as when I was not."

'Without before or after' – our outer lives are well and truly attached to time as a rule. But if we can drop our clinging to past and future and no longer need to depend on them for our sense of duration, of security, of busy bustling life, then we can live in this instant now and pay full attention to what is, rather than to what has been or is yet to come. "For *not* to be concerned with the present is the hallmark of evasion" says Harry Williams. He quotes: "'Behold *now* is the accepted time. Behold *now* is the day of salvation.'"

Critics of such statements as Eckhart's might say that this is escapism, an attempt to evade the world. But Eckhart did not mean this. Rather he meant an entry into life in such a balanced way that this present Now is always full of grace, of equanimity and of ease. He meant living right *in* life, so that whatever happens we are living our lives in a universal way, always working in the direction of where the universal is alive.

"God is not a destroyer of anything that is good. He is a fulfiller. He is a perfecter of nature and never one to overthrow it. His grace will not negate nature but perfect it until it is at its best."

"God creates all things in an ever-present Now", he said, meaning that this instant now is the only instant when creation is possible. The past has gone, the future is still in our heads. He also meant that the whole action of God's continuous creation is timeless, outside time, and has no reference to our limited experience of time.

"The soul's day and God's day are different . . . a day, whether six or seven ago – or more than six thousand years ago – is just as near to the present as yesterday . . . and that is why I say, this day all things are of equal rank. To talk about the world as being made by God tomorrow, yesterday, would be talking nonsense. God makes the world and all things in this very instant. Time gone a thousand years ago is now as present and near to God as this very instant. The soul who is in this present now, in her the Father bears his one-begotten Son and in the same birth the soul is born back into God. It is one birth; as fast as he is reborn into God the Father is begetting his only Son in her."

And in quantum physics we read: "Since all particles can move forwards or backwards in time, just as they can move left and right in space, it does not make sense to impose a one-way flow of time. . . . In the words of Louis de Broglie: 'In space-time, everything which for each of us constitutes the past, the present and the future *is given en bloc* ['in this very instant']. . . . Each observer, as his time passes, discovers, so to speak, new slices of space-time which appear to him as successive aspects of the material world, though in reality the ensemble of events constituting space-time exist prior to his knowledge of them'." (Capra, *The Tao of Physics*.)

"*Now* is time and place *in itself*", said Eckhart. "While man has [is attached to] time and place, number and quantity, he is not as he should be, is not just, and God is remote and not his own. . . . Now is not a bit of time nor a part of time. It is rather a taste of time, a relative of time, an end of time. . . .

"Time is what keeps the light from reaching us. There is no greater obstacle than time. And not only time but impermanence, not only impermanent things but impermanent affections; not only impermanent affections, but the very taint and smell of time."

By these passages we can see that what Eckhart regards as our highest consciousness must be oned with the God-ground beyond time and space.

"Nothing hinders the soul's knowledge of God as much as time and space, for time and space are fragments, whereas God is one. And therefore, if the soul is to know God, it must know him above time and outside of space; for God is neither this nor that, as are these manifold things. God is One."

Erwin Schrödinger (discoverer of the Schrödinger wave equation), implying that we are at one and the same time God and creature, echoes Eckhart when he says: "It is not possible that this unity of knowledge, feeling and choice which you call *your own* should have sprung into being from nothingness at a given moment not so long ago; rather, this knowledge, feeling and choice are essentially eternal and unchangeable and numerically *one* in all men, indeed in all sensitive beings. But not in *this* sense – that *you* are a part, a piece, of an eternal and infinite being – an aspect or modification of it . . . for then we should have the same baffling question: which part, which aspect are *you*? What, objectively, differentiates it from others? No; but inconceivable as it seems to ordinary reason, you – and all other conscious beings as such – are all in all. Hence this life of yours which you are living is not merely a piece of the entire existence, but it is in a certain sense the *whole*; only this whole is not so constituted that it can be surveyed in one single glance."

Time and space were so important to Eckhart that he spoke and wrote a great deal about these two aspects of existence and some of his statements not only baffled his hearers – as well as many generations since – but also led the Church to look with some suspicion at what he was trying to say. And indeed it is not always clear. The best way of approaching the whole question is to follow Eckhart's suggestion, which is to think of human beings as made 'between one and two'. The one is 'eternity, ever alone and without variation'; the two is 'time, changing and given to multiplication'.

". . . the soul in her highest consciousness touches timelessness, meaning God, while her lower consciousness being in contact with time makes her subject to change and caught by bodily things, which pull her down. Could the soul know God as well as the angels do she would never have come into body. If she could know God without the world the world would not have been made for her sake. The world was contrived on her account for training and bracing the eye of the soul to endure divine light. The sunshine falling on the earth is dimmed first in the atmosphere and diffused on various things, for no human eye can support the sun. And even so the light of God is over strong and bright for the soul's eye to bear, unless it is fixed in space and given up to matter and to the reflection of God, which accustom it to dwelling in the light divine.

"St Augustine says: 'God is not far off nor is he long in coming.' If you want not to be far from God nor to wait long for him, then go straight to him, for in him a thousand years are but as yesterday when it is past. I also say that in God there is neither sorrow, nor crying, nor any pain. If you will be rid of pain and suffering, stop where you are and turn to God – but only to him.

"I have often said: he who seeks God while seeking other things [such as intellectual explanations] will never find God. But if someone seeks only God, he finds God – and never quite alone, for all that God can give he finds together with God. If you seek God for your own advantage, then in truth you are not looking for God at all.

'Turn to God – but only to him' – Eckhart was against analysing and defining God or much speculation about him.

"If you ask a good man: Why do you seek God? – he will answer, 'Because he is God.' Why do you seek the truth? 'Because it is the truth.' Why do you seek justice? 'Because it is justice.' Such people's attitude is the right one. All things that are in time have a reason. Thus when someone asks a man: Why are you eating? – he will answer, 'To gain strength.' Why are you sleeping? 'For the same reason.' And so with everything in time. But if someone asked a good man: Why do you love God? – he would reply, 'I do not know, because he *is* God.' Why do you love truth? 'For the sake of truth.' Why do you love justice? 'For the sake of justice.' Why do you love goodness? 'Because of goodness.' Why are you living? 'Upon my soul, I don't know. But I am happy to be alive!'"

The acceptance of all things just as they are and the living of them – what a respite from doubt and fear! A short Zen verse says:

When sitting, just sit.
When moving, just move.
Above all, don't wobble.

Eckhart, now become famous as a great teacher and also a busy administrator – travelling all over his domain on foot, as was the custom of the time, throughout north Germany, Holland, Bohemia, Switzerland and France – was summoned to Cologne to hold the same chair which had once been honoured by Albert the Great. There could be no refusal and undoubtedly none was considered since such a position was one of the greatest honours bestowable on any scholar.

At a date unknown but not earlier than 1322 Eckhart, then, went to Cologne. But here he ran straight into trouble of the worst sort. He was a Dominican and the Archbishop of Cologne was a Franciscan, harsh, narrow and elderly. He had been responsible for the burning and drowning of many members of the 'heretical' sects which were at that time defying the power of the Church. He detested any teaching which carried even the faintest breath of unorthodoxy and so a mystic such as Eckhart – and a Dominican into the bargain (for the antagonism between the two Orders was still strong) – presented a threat which only extreme measures could remove.

In 1326, consequently, the Archbishop began proceedings against Eckhart in the judgement chambers of the Inquisition. His accusation was that Eckhart was teaching dangerous doctrines to the common people in their own tongue. Such accusations were based at least partly on Eckhart's understanding of the Godhead as being beyond even the Trinity:

"In the unborn essence He is essential essence without personality: essence self-manifest as impersonal being. . . . In the essence the Father loses his Fatherhood completely; nor is there any Father at all."

And: ". . . the soul enters the unity of the Holy Trinity, but it may become even more blessed by going further, to the barren Godhead, of which the Trinity is a revelation."

Such statements probably made the Archbishop's fury swell. Eckhart also challenged the view then upheld by the Church that man was the greatest of God's creatures, by saying that when we are in the highest consciousness we see that "God gives to everything alike, and as flowing forth from God things are all equal; angels, man, and creatures all proceed from God alike in their first emanation. To take things in their primal emanation is to take them all alike. If here in time they are alike, in God in timelessness they are much more so. Any flea as it is in God is nobler than the highest of angels is in himself. Things are all the same in God: they are God himself."

And: "God delights so in this likeness or identity that he pours out his whole nature, his whole substance into it. His pleasure is as great, to take a simile, as that of a horse turned loose in a lush meadow, giving vent to his horse-nature by galloping full-tilt about the field: he enjoys it, and it is his nature. So it is with God. It is his pleasure and rapture to discover likeness, and he pours his entire nature and his being into this likeness – for he is this likeness himself."

This teaching may have infuriated the rigidly pious Archbishop, yet to accuse such a renowned and honoured figure as Eckhart of virtual heresy was still an unheard-of action. Eckhart replied, with dignity and courage, that although in fact he was answerable only to the University of Paris and the Pope, he would, for the sake of the good name of the Dominican Order, defend himself before the local inquisitors.

The three inquisitors appointed to hear him included two Franciscans, one of whom was Italian and the other Dutch, while the third inquisitor was a native of Cologne. Not one of them was equipped with the knowledge and understanding necessary to prove a case against Eckhart, and he, perhaps with understandable gleefulness, showed up their ignorance of the Scriptures time and again.

It is because of this trial and the extension of it that historians have been able to piece together the sermons and treatises which Eckhart himself wrote, as distinct from those written under his influence by other people. Some one hundred and eight statements, many still preserved but some lost, were held against him, either then or later on. At the first trial in Cologne, the accusations were mainly shown to be ignorant misinterpretations of the Bible and Eckhart proved with ease that what he taught was entirely in accord with Biblical sources.

Nevertheless, the Inquisition was out to catch him and catch him it did. Another list of 'heretical' passages taken from his commentary on St John's Gospel was produced. The Vicar-General of the Dominican Order intervened on behalf of Eckhart; not only was he overruled by the Archbishop, but the Archbishop actually took proceedings against him too.

At this point other eminent men and prominent Dominicans rushed forward to testify on Eckhart's behalf. They loved him, he was their teacher and brother, and his trial was incredible to all. But the Inquisition, although having to scrape the barrel, at last produced two Dominicans of notoriously bad character (one of whom was even already excommunicated!) to testify against him.

By that time the best part of a year had slipped by (perhaps our own lengthy legal delays are not so unusual after all) and Eckhart protested to the Pope about the slow nature of the trial. He appealed for his innocence to be established and in February 1327 made a solemn declaration to his own Order that he was not a heretic, pointing out that the accusations against him were based on misunderstandings and distortions. He also declared that if any real fallacy in either faith or morals should be found in any of his writings or in anything he had said, publicly or in private, then that, whatever it was, should be considered not said or written. This declaration was read out in Latin and testified to by a notary.

Although Eckhart's appeal was to the Pope himself, the enraged and embittered Archbishop would not allow it to be sent. But the Pope had now begun to take an interest in it all anyway, and a fresh hearing was arranged to take place in Avignon. A panel of theologians was appointed to look at the whole case and they produced a new list of suspicious articles and sermons. Cardinal Jacques Fournier, later to be Pope Benedict XII, was the principal judge, and he was a learned scholar and theologian, able at least to form a better judgement on Eckhart's teaching than those before him.

By coincidence, he was at the same time preparing a case against the Englishman, William of Ockham, a Franciscan. Both William and Eckhart were to some extent confined to Avignon, although the word prisoner may be too strong for their situation. Ockham, however, had no sympathy for his fellow detainee, considering Eckhart's ideas to be plainly mad.

But he was suffering from a sense of outrage at the time, believing that the Papacy favoured Dominicans over Franciscans. He was soon to escape from Avignon, bringing with him for posterity some exact knowledge of the charges against Eckhart.

Early in the next year, 1328, the Archbishop, no doubt longing to get his teeth into Eckhart again, wrote to the Pope urging him to come to a decision about the whole affair. The Pope wrote back to say that Eckhart was dead.

Nobody knows exactly how he died, or when or where. It was at some time before the thirtieth of April of that year and the presumption is that he died in Avignon, although he might have been on his way back to Cologne. He was in fact already dead when Ockham escaped, although Ockham was not aware of this. There was, however, no question of foul play. Eckhart was by then an old man, his life had been a hard one, and his trial a matter of great anxiety and sorrow.

In the following year, the Pope (John XXII) issued a bull in which fifteen Latin and two German works of Eckhart's were condemned as heretical, and eleven other Latin works termed 'dangerous and suspect of heresy'. The bull ended by saying that just before his death Eckhart had revoked all of his works which might be considered heretical (the same sort of statement as he made to the Dominicans in Cologne). Because of this statement he therefore escaped a posthumous excommunication. Nevertheless the condemnation of his beliefs as heretical had a fatal effect on his reputation. After the deaths of his two chief pupils, Tauler and Suso, a silence fell over him and all his works although, luckily, they were kept intact for the most part by the devoted nuns and monks of the Dominican Order. The seventeenth-century mystic, Johann Scheffler, who, under the name of Angelus Silesius, wrote verse based on Eckhart's teaching, was virtually the only person of renown to show any interest in him until the nineteenth century.

Poor Eckhart! He was spared by death the knowledge that his works were finally condemned, but it must have been exceptionally hard for an old man such as he, who had spent his whole life in caring for the spiritual welfare of others and in giving out all that he had discovered of an inner life, as well as loving the Church and serving her as he thought faithfully and well, to be judged, first by an ignorant assortment of inquisition accusers, and then by a Pope who himself, later on, stood trial for heresy and was excommunicated.

Eckhart's love for people had expressed itself in an unsparing effort to help them to realise that "the eye by which I see God is the same eye by which he sees me. My eye and the eye of God are one eye, one vision, one knowledge, and one love."

To his congregations he would say such things as: "Our Lord says to every living soul, 'I became man for you. If you do not become God for me, you do me wrong'."

"Begin with yourself and *abandon yourself*! In truth, if you do not first flee from yourself, wherever else you may flee you will find hindrance and trouble, wherever it be. . . . Indeed, if a man had given up a kingdom or the whole world, but kept himself, he had abandoned nothing."

"God expects but one thing of you, and that is that you should come out of yourself in so far as you are a created being and let God be God in you."

"Many people imagine *here* to have creaturely being, and divine being *yonder*. That is not so. By that many are deceived. A man beholds God in this life in the same perfection, and is blessed in exactly the same way, as in the after life."

"God is near to us, but we are far from him. God is in, we are out; God is at home, we are strangers."

Such a way of putting things may have puzzled many of his parishioners. But they loved him and he them, for his feet were always on the ground, however high his heart soared: "As I have often said, even if a man were in rapture like St Paul, and knew a sick man who needed some soup from him, I should think it far better you left the rapture for love and served the needy man in greater love."

And he tempered his own difficult ideas by giving simple advice: "You must find out what God wants most from you; for men are by no means all called to follow one way . . . if you find your nearest way is not through many external works and great pains and privileges – which really do not matter so very much, unless a man is specially impelled to them by God and has the strength to do these things well and without disturbing his inner life – if, then, you do not find anything like that in yourself, be quite content and do not worry about it. Now you might say: If this really does not matter, why then have these things been done by so many saintly forbears of ours? Now think: Our Lord gave them *this* way, but also the strength to see that they could carry it through, and this was his good pleasure for *them* . . . but God has not attached salvation to any particular way."

To end a chapter on Eckhart with one of his own sayings is to be tempted to start all over again. But instead, to really conclude, here are some verses from a poem called 'A Grain of Mustard-Seed' which, according to M. O'C. Walshe, is quite likely to be by Eckhart himself. It certainly seems to breathe his spirit directly to us.

> The threefold clasp
> we cannot grasp,
> the circle's span
> no mind can scan:
> for here's a mystery fathomless.
> Check and mate,
> time, form, estate!
> The wondrous ring
> holds everything,
> its central point stands motionless.
>
> The peak sublime
> deedless climb
> if you are wise!
> Your way then lies
> Through desert very strange to see,
> so deep, so wide,
> no bound's descried.
> This desert's bare
> of *Then* or *There*
> in modeless singularity.
>
> This desert place
> no foot did pace,
> no creature mind
> ingress can find.
> It *is*, yet truly none knows what.

'Tis there, 'tis here,
'tis far, 'tis near,
'tis high, 'tis low,
yet all we know
is: *This* it's not and *That* it's not.

The Cloud of Unknowing

The mystery surrounding the author of *The Cloud* has never yet been solved. His name lies undiscovered. The only real fact established about him – and it is deduced from language and reference – is that he lived in the latter part of the fourteenth century in the East Midlands of England. Evelyn Underhill thought that he must have been a monk, but opinion now believes it most likely that he was a priest with a large parish.

He himself may have remained anonymous but his writings have had a more penetrating effect on Christian mysticism than almost any others, and are quoted perhaps the most frequently; in particular his major work, *The Cloud of Unknowing*.

In many ways he shared the same treasure-house of insights as Eckhart, but his way of writing is simple and direct, so that he gives us the results of his highest intuitions in an easy, simple, vivid style as though they were everyday experiences, the next practical steps that we should take. And indeed practice is the essence of his teaching – the actual ways we should follow to find our own reality. He has a particular talent for sensing the struggling bewilderment of the beginner and for advising him with a calm practicality which makes him one of the most realistic of all the mystics. If such direct instruction in the methods of contemplation had stayed in the forefront of Christian life, one wonders what Christianity would have been like today.

The writings of Dionysius the Areopagite were the words of his teacher, and he bases his own inspired works almost entirely on the *Mystical Theology* of Dionysius – a mystic whom Eckhart too was considerably influenced by – which work he translated into English. He called the *Mystical Theology, Denis Hid Divinity – Hid Divinity* meaning the ultimate mystery of the God-ground and *Denis* being Dionysius. *Denis Hid Divinity* is a short but powerful instruction on how to be oned with God. It describes how all things of divinity 'be covered and hid under the sovereign-shining darkness of wisest silence . . . in a manner that is always invisible and ungropable – fulfilling with sovereign clarity all those that enter into it by closing the eyes of the mind'. It emphasises the timelessness of the God-ground by pointing out that it will not be found by unwise men who 'be fastened on knowing and loving of these things that be knowable and have a beginning'. The Divinity is beyond the knowable and beyond time, and yet 'clearly he [God] appears open, not to all, but to them only which pass above all bad and good being things and which come above all holy names and which forsake all divine lights and all heavenly sounds and words and enter with affection into darkness, where verily he is . . . above all'.

This essentially was the message of Dionysius – that man must let go his attachment to the things of this world in order to find the divinity, or God-ground, this 'most luminous' darkness that 'shines brighter than light' and 'illuminates with splendours of unapproachable beauty', and which is beyond all naming and thinking. And the way to let go is by 'will and by love'.

In the *Cloud* this is tellingly put: "For of all other creatures and their works, yes, and of the works of God's self, may a man through grace have full head of knowing, and well he can think of them: but of God himself can no man think. And therefore I would leave all that thing which I can think, and choose to my love that thing that I cannot think. For why; He may well be loved but not thought. By love he may be gotten and holden; but by thought never. And therefore, although it be good sometimes to think of the kindness and the worthiness of God in special; and although it be a light and a part of contemplation: yet nevertheless in this work it shall be cast down and covered with a cloud of forgetting. And you shall step above it stalwartly, but listily [yearningly] with a devout and a pleasing stirring of love, and try to pierce that darkness above you. And smite upon that thick cloud of unknowing with a sharp dart of longing love; and go not away from there for anything that befalls."

All through the Middle Ages Dionysius was believed to be St Paul's disciple of the same name, and so his work was regarded as authoritative and was held in great respect. It was only in the Renaissance that his identity was doubted and recent evidence has proved the St Paul connection impossible. It is now thought that Dionysius was a Syrian monk of the sixth century. But whatever his origin, nothing is detracted from the sublime understanding which fertilised the seed of Christianity and brought it to flower so mysteriously and wonderfully in the Middle Ages. The inspiration he gave to such mystics as St Bernard, Meister Eckhart, Jan van Ruysbroeck and a host of others up to St John of the Cross and St Theresa of Avila, can never be evaluated.

His greatest spiritual heir was the author of the *Cloud*, who took one of Dionysius' sentences as the key to his own understanding – 'the most godly knowing of God is that which is known by unknowing'. He calls his book *The Cloud of Unknowing* because of his own same experience and conviction that the God-ground cannot be discovered by way of knowing *about* it, but only by unknowing – by putting down all that is known and becoming innocent and ignorant. This ignorance is not lack of *real* knowledge; for just in this dark area of contemplation, where all knowledge about particular things and all feelings cease, man comes to an infinitely greater understanding, in which 'he is well taught to understand all things bodily or ghostly [spiritual]' – that is, a new clarity of knowledge in which he sees all things afresh so that he is enlightened by all that he sees.

The author of the *Cloud* was a true mystic in that he was practical as well as contemplative, down to earth as well as soaring upwards. He knew well the difficulties of the way he proposed. Consequently he taught various exercises which any practitioner could use to open up to the God-ground, so that it could then be recognised and realised within. He believed fervently that this *could* be done – 'trust steadfastly that there is such a perfect meekness as I speak of, and that it may be come to through grace in this life' – and that it *should* be done.

"Lift up your heart unto God with a meek stirring of love;

and mean himself and none of his goods . . . so that nothing works in your wit, nor in your will, but only himself. And do that in you to forget all the creatures that God ever made and the works of them . . . this is the work that most pleases God . . . all men living on earth be wonderfully helped by this work, you know not how. Even those in purgatory are eased of their pain by virtue of this work [purgatory being a here and now state of mind]. You yourself are cleansed and purified by no work so much. And yet it is the lightest work of all, when a soul is helped with grace in eager activity, and soonest done."

This then was the urgent task which all men should accomplish – or, rather, not all – for the author of the *Cloud* was well aware that the majority of people, Christian and non-Christian alike, were not in the least concerned, any more than they are today, 'to see as God sees', but much preferred to live and move with the crowd. To such as these the author requested that his work should not be presented at all. He saw danger in the ignorant attempting to carry out his exercises and he expected that any who undertook them would have become accustomed to self-discipline and meditation first. Here is a point on which all religions agree. Any real practice demands the purification of oneself at the beginning – and by purification is meant a heightened awareness of the nature of who one is and the results of one's actions.

The practical training which the author of the *Cloud* offers is remarkably close to some of the techniques practised by the religious of both East and West today. His practices are very relevant to our condition, bringing us away from the horizontal world of ever-changing phenomena and taking us to the deeper and more profound reality which we come to know as the centre and heart of ourselves.

These practices are contained more concisely in another book he wrote called *The Book of Privy Counselling* than in the *Cloud*. Whereas the *Cloud* is certainly written by a young man, *The Book of Privy Counselling* shows a maturity of understanding perhaps even greater than in the *Cloud*, although it lacks some of the *Cloud*'s memorable and sublime prose.

The Book of Privy Counselling begins, then, in this way:

"When you go apart by yourself in solitude, do not think about what you will be doing afterwards, and put away all good thoughts as well as evil ones; and do not pray with words unless you feel you really must. Or if you do have something to say, do not look at how much or how little it is, nor what it means, whether it is orison or psalm, hymn, anthem or any other prayer, general or specific, silently formed within or spoken out loud. And look that nothing remains in your conscious mind but a naked intent stretching unto God, not clothed in any particular thought *about* God – what he is like in himself or in any of his works – but *only that he is as he is*. Let him be so, I pray you, and do not make him otherwise. Pry no further into him by subtlety of intelligence; let faith be your solid ground. That naked intent, emptied of ideas and grounded in very faith, shall be to your thoughts and feelings a naked thought and a blind feeling of your own being; as if, with your whole heart, you said to God: 'That which I am, good Lord, I offer to you, without any looking at the nature of your being, but only that you are as you are, without any more.'

"Let that quiet darkness be the whole of your mind and a mirror for you. Think no more about your personality than I bid you do of God's, so that you are oned with him just as you are, without any fragmenting or disturbance of your mind. For he is your beingness, and in him you are what you are, not only because he is the cause and being of all that is, but because he is in you both *your* cause and *your* being. And therefore be aware of God in your contemplation in the same way as you are aware of yourself, and of yourself in the same way as you are of God; that he is as he is and you are as you are; so that then your thoughts are not scattered or separated but are oned in him who is the totality – yet not forgetting this difference, that he is your being but you are not his. For although it is so that all things exist in him because he is their cause and their being; yet in himself he alone is his own cause and his own being. For as nothing can exist without him, so he cannot be without himself. He is beingness, both to himself and to all. And in that way only is he separated from all that is created, in that he is unconditioned being. And in that he is both one and all, all things are one in him and all things have their being in him, as he is the being of all.

"So it is that your thoughts and your feelings will be oned with him by grace without separation, as long as all seeking and curiosity about the particular qualities of your blind being or of his are put far away. Let your thought be naked and your feeling unattached and you just simply as you are, so that the touch of God may fill you with the realisation of him just as he is, even though it may be blindly and partially as yet, so that your longing desire will be evermore working.

"Look up then happily and say to the Lord, either out loud or within your heart, 'That which I am, Lord, I offer to you, for you are it.' And be aware nakedly, plainly and strongly, that you are as you are."

The acceptance of a fact is not at all the same as an explanation of it. Allowing ourselves to be one with Reality is not the same thing as theorising about it. The one great instruction which emerges from this passage is that we should experience a 'naked' reaching – a dropping away of thought and feeling, idea and image, so that Reality can be known as it is. Why is this 'simple' task so hard for us?

One of man's heaviest burdens is his sense of existential insecurity. The world seems to run its course regardless of our interest in it, leaving us to get on as best we can while it goes its predetermined and uncaring way. Deeply conscious of doubt, isolation (for this is the full terror, that when we suffer we suffer alone while the rest of the world goes about its usual business), insecurity, and the impermanence of all objects, relationships and situations, we fight back, trying to build up our own sort of world for ourselves. But to do that we must first chop it to pieces, accepting only those bits which please us and rejecting the rest; so that in the end life ceases to have much, if any, objective reality for us and becomes merely the battleground for our loves and hates, likes and dislikes. This makes us perpetually restless, always in a state of becoming – of adding to our person in one way or another – and always afraid that what we have will be taken from us.

And quite apart from our own chopping actions, life itself seems to be divided into many compartments, with many roles to play, such as family, career, politics, finances, personal life and so on. These often conflict with one another because the same person may be playing different roles and leading different lives all, so to speak, jammed together. Stress and contradiction arise because people become over-involved, and identify with their roles and images and lose the meaning of living, of naked being. Is there such a thing as this naked being at all? We start asking such questions when we have lost the sense of the wholeness of life, when we are immersed in disharmony and disintegration, when our sense of identity is derived only from the outside.

We 'keep up appearances' – how well that phrase describes the many masks we put on. When we derive our identity only from our interaction with other people, we then need others to accept and reaffirm our existence and we often spend considerable time and energy striving for this recognition. Our derived identity, made up of all our many appearances, becomes our most precious possession – without it we think we would cease to be. This is why physical death brings such great fear; it implies the loss of everything we have identified with.

But in this teaching we are asked to develop a consciousness that does not wear masks or have appearances; that does not even *evaluate*, but simply accepts that there *is* a God-ground and it is as it is; and that when masks are taken off and roles are dropped, we are as we are. In the profound acceptance that existence *is*, lies the miracle cure for all the ills which rack us. To live life in such a way that it is just as it is, is to allow all things to exist in their own right without a shred of our judgement or comparison projected on to them. When our projections no longer colour the world around us, the objective truth of reality can shine through, convincing us that an unimaginable wonder exists as the essential beingness of all things – that it exists whether we notice or not, and that in this just-as-it-isness we can come finally to rest.

'A naked thought and a blind feeling of your own being' – the author of the *Cloud* did not mean anything complicated by this but something so simple that for many of us it is *too* simple – too many masks have to be dropped. Certainly that clear-sighted mystic found it so in his day, and he bemoans the fact that people say, "my writing . . . is so hard and so high, so curious and so clever, that it can scarcely be thought about by the subtlest or most quick-witted man or woman in this life". With a sharpened tongue, he continues: "For I cannot hold anyone too dull or too simple that he is not able to think and feel that he is – not *what* he is but *that* he is. For this is plainly possible for the stupidest cow, or the most unreasonable beast – to feel their own being. How much more then is it possible for man, who is endowed with reason above all other animals, to think and feel his own being?"

He would have been in sympathy perhaps with the Indian sage, Ramana Maharshi, who thought that the feeling of 'I' was the basis of all the scriptures. One of the questions continually being put to him was, 'How can I find out who I am?' With the sharpness of the author of the *Cloud*, he answered once, "If you don't know who you are, who else can tell you?" for he felt that people muddle themselves up with conceptual thinking and that if they could only become simple they would see the truth in a moment. And in the same fashion, Bankei, a Japanese Zen master of the seventeenth century, announced: 'The birthless mind [naked being] is possessed by all and none truly strays from it. It is that you turn it into something else. When you are not in it – when you sell it, so to speak, for worthless things you happen to be attached to – then you go astray.'

"'I exist' is the only permanent, self-evident experience of everyone", said Ramana Maharshi. "Nothing else is so self-evident as 'I am'. What people call 'self-evidence', viz., the experience they get through the senses, is far from self-evident. . . . 'I am' is reality. I am *this* or *that* is unreal . . . God exists in 'I am' in every thing and every being."

Referring to the basic insecurity and consequent suffering of ego-centred man, the *Cloud*'s author, in characteristically robust language, advises him to:

"Take good, gracious God as he is, flat and plain as a plaster, and lay it to your sick self as you are. Or, putting it another way, bear up your sick self as you are and try to touch good, gracious God as he is, the touching of whom is endless health . . . much more will you then be made whole of your sickness by this high heavenly touching of his own being. Step up then stoutly and taste of that medicine. Bear up your sick self to gracious God as he is, without any curiosity or special thinking about all the qualities that belong to the being of yourself or of God, whether they be clean or wretched, full of grace or natural, godly or manly. It matters not to you, but only that your blind beholding of your naked being be gladly borne up in the joyous activity of love, to be knitted and oned in grace and spirit to the precious being of God in himself, only as he is, without more."

The *Cloud*'s author was concerned to talk only about the actual *experience* of knowing the God-ground as oneself, he was not concerned with any theology about it. He was aware that that particular clarity of non-dual being is essential to man's sanity and courage. If it is not experienced then faith is bound to be uncertain and the security of existence imperilled. How do we arrive at such an experience?

It is discovered, say all religions, partly through the strange and mysterious *sense* of the God-ground which pulls us towards itself as though towards a magnet; and partly by opening ourselves by means of techniques, such as meditation or silent prayer, so that the mind is stilled and words no longer enslave us. One such technique is suggested in the *Cloud*:

"If you would have a naked intent direct unto God without any other cause than himself, and if you would have this intent lapped and folded in one word so that you should more easily keep it in your mind, take but a little word of one syllable: it is better than two for the shorter it is the more it accords with the Spirit. And such a word is this word 'God' or this word 'love'. Choose which you will, or another, whichever appeals to you of one syllable. And fasten this word to your heart, so that it never leaves you whatever befalls.

"This word shall be your shield and your spear, whether you ride in peace or in war. With this word you shall beat on this cloud and this darkness above you. With this word you shall smite down all manner of thoughts under the cloud of forgetting. Insomuch, that if any thought presses upon you to ask of you what you are doing, answer with no more words but with just this one word. And if your questioning mind wishes to expand on the meaning of that word or to tell you the conditions of it, answer it that you will have it whole and not broken or undone. And if you will hold fast to this purpose, be sure your thoughts will no longer trouble you. And why? Because you have not allowed them to feed on that sweet meditation of God."

Here, then, is the teaching of mantra, the use of a word or

syllable to calm the restless mind and bring it to a state of one-pointed stillness. It has been used for many centuries in the Orthodox Church, as well as being a main technique in Hinduism and Buddhism. Those who know *The Way of a Pilgrim*, the true story of a nineteenth-century Russian who was given by his spiritual teacher a prayer, 'Lord Jesus Christ, have mercy on me', to repeat within his mind all the time, will remember how he started doing it several times a day for half an hour at a time and how, after a bit, he was able to picture the beating of his heart and could put into it and draw from it, the Prayer of Jesus. "When drawing the air in I looked in spirit into my heart and said, 'Lord Jesus Christ', and when breathing out again, I said, 'Have mercy on me'. I did this . . . for an hour at a time, then for two hours, then for as long as I could, and in the end almost all day long. . . .

"When about three weeks had passed I felt a pain in my heart and then a most delightful warmth, as well as consolation and peace . . . From this time I began to have from time to time a number of different feelings in my heart and mind. Sometimes my heart would feel as though it were bubbling with joy, such lightness, freedom and consolation were in it. Sometimes I felt a burning love for Jesus Christ and for all God's creatures. Sometimes my eyes brimmed over with tears of thankfulness to God, who was so merciful to me, a wretched sinner. Sometimes my understanding, which had been so stupid before, was given so much light that I could easily grasp and dwell upon matters of which up to now I had not been able to think at all. Sometimes that sense of a warm gladness in my heart spread throughout my whole being and I was deeply moved as the fact of the presence of God everywhere was brought home to me. Sometimes by calling upon the name of Jesus I was overwhelmed with bliss, and now I knew the meaning of the words '*The Kingdom of God is within you*'.

"After spending five months in this lonely life of prayer and such happiness as this, I grew so used to the Prayer that I went on with it all the time. In the end I felt it going on of its own accord within my mind and in the depths of my heart, without any urging on my part. Not only when I was awake, but even during sleep just the same thing went on. Nothing broke into it and it never stopped even for a single moment, whatever I might be doing. My soul was always giving thanks to God and my heart melted away with unceasing happiness."

'If you would have a naked intent unto God' – the author of the *Cloud* believed that the chief condition necessary for a mantra to work is a strong desire to realise the depths of the God-ground. If this is genuinely felt, the name or word will be taken with true longing and love of such a way. This brings about a purification of the mind and a transparency within it. By constantly repeating the name – sometimes with breathing and a feeling of the God-ground in the heart, as the Pilgrim practised – consciousness of an ineffable state grows. That consciousness fills the mind and senses with a very sweet and happy feeling of integration, which eradicates all the crowding thoughts below it.

When repeating the name (the little Hindu sound of 'Om', representing the totality of the universe, is also both easy and suitable), if we are conscious that we are repeating the name of that which is already within us as our true being and existence, and keep this central fact in our heart all the time, then the practice will gradually make us properly aware of that existence within us. At the beginning we are not aware of this, but may intellectually accept the idea that it is so and so we repeat the name. But this idea grows into real and intimate experience as the practice itself becomes real and not just a pastime. Full surrender to the words takes us beyond words, just as full surrender to the form of God takes us beyond forms. It is when we do not surrender that the form still remains a form and the word a word. So God's name and form are meditated on only in order to reach the ultimate Reality which is the being of everything.

"Under whatever name or form one may worship the Absolute Reality," said Ramana Maharshi, "it is only a means for realising It without name and form. That alone is true realisation wherein one knows oneself in relation to that Reality, attains peace and realises one's identity with It."

'This word shall be your shield and your sword', said the author of the *Cloud*. Our world is not, for most of us, a quiet meditation hall. Busy and distracted, we tend to let practices slip, or we find ourselves in situations where the practice is not possible and we grow fretful and anxious. But a word can be repeated in the mind in any circumstances, can be held on to as though to a rope in times of great disturbance, can bring the concentration back when it has wandered, and can be used with love in any peaceful moment. The *Cloud*'s author says:

"A man or woman, terrified by some impending disaster which is taking him to the limits of his own resources, is driven by panic and needs to make a great cry or prayer for help. Yet how? Surely not in many words, nor even in one word of two syllables. Why is that? Because he has no time to do more than burst out in a great and desperate cry of, for instance, 'Fire!' or 'Out!' or 'Help!'

"And just as this one little word 'fire!' pierces and alerts the ears of others, so does a little word of one syllable when not only is it spoken and thought, but when it surges up out of the depths of a man's spirit . . . pierce the ears of Almighty God more than does any long psalm mindlessly mumbled in the teeth. And so it is written that short prayer pierces heaven.

"And why does it pierce heaven, this little short prayer of one syllable? Surely because it is the prayer of a man's whole being, prayed with all the height and depth and length and breadth of his spirit. It is high because it is the most mighty prayer of his heart. It is deep because in this little syllable is gathered all the awareness of the spirit; it is long because, were it to go on feeling in this way it would cry out always; and it is broad because it wills for all others what it wills for itself."

The author of the *Cloud* gives us surely the most effective mantra – one little word. The Pilgrim used seven, but the poet, Tennyson, used only two – his own name! He said:

"A kind of waking trance I have frequently had quite up from boyhood, when I have been all alone. This has generally come upon me through repeating my own name two or three times to myself silently, till all at once, as it were out of the intensity of the consciousness of individuality, the individuality itself seemed to dissolve and fade away into boundless being, and this not a confused state but the clearest of the clearest, the surest of the surest, the weirdest of the weirdest, utterly beyond words, where death was an almost laughable impossibility, the loss of personality (if so it were) seeming no extinction but the only true life."

'Hear all sounds as mantra' says Tibetan Buddhism. In this

sense, mantra, according to John Blofeld, signifies divine melody. And indeed if one stops interfering with noise by categorising it or preferring one sound to another, the resultant intermingling of sounds can really seem a symphony of the world. We usually regard any particular noise as an interference. John Blofeld recalls that when he was living in Bangkok his meditation in the early hours of the morning was constantly interrupted by learners driving motor-tricycle taxis in low gear round a square below his window. 'By mentally converting the horrid din into the rattle of the Lama's hand-drums heard above the noise of a cataract, I made it most helpful to my meditation.'

Perhaps the author of the *Cloud* would agree that when we are unable to hear the mantra, our chosen word, as for instance when we are distraught and the strength of our feelings seems to obliterate the practice of saying it, then we can look around us and find that we are surrounded by natural substitutes – the waves on the shore, wind in the trees, the beating of rain – and such sounds can act most powerfully in healing the mind and bringing it back to one-pointedness as long as the surrender is *fully made*. It must be a 'naked' surrender, in that descriptions such as the colour of the waves or their regularity are not considered in any way relevant, but only the fact that the waves *are*, that the sea *is*, that the rain *is*, that sound *is*. When sound is sound and no longer thought of as disturbing noise then *all* sound, including heavy traffic, football matches, and our neighbour's barking dog, can be regarded as part of the 'isness' of life, creating a music of their own.

Indeed that very action of accepting the 'isness' of existence is regarded by the author of the *Cloud* as an essential meditation, and he describes it in *The Book of Privy Counselling*:

"You know right well now that in this work you shall no more look to the characteristics of the being of God than to the characteristics of the being of yourself. For there is no name, nor feeling, nor apprehending so close to the timelessness of God as that which may be had, seen and felt in the blind and loving awareness of this word *is*. For if you say good or fair or sweet, merciful or righteous, wise or all-knowing, mighty or all-mighty, knowledge or wisdom, might or strength, love or charity, or whatever else you say of God – all of it underlies and is contained in this little word *is*. And if you added a hundred thousand such sweet words as these – good, fair and all these other – yet you would not add to this little word *is*. And if you said none of them, you would have taken nothing from it. . . . And so, with all idle curiosity left far behind, do worship God with all that you are, just as you are, and surrender to him just as he is, for he is the blissful beingness both of himself and of you. And so shall you knittingly [bindingly], in a manner that is marvellous, surrender to God within himself, because all that you are you have from him and his very essence is yours. And although you had a beginning in your physical creation – before which you were nothing – yet your true being has always been in him without beginning and shall always be in him without ending, as he himself is.

"And so I often cry this one thing: 'Do worship God with all that you are and help all mankind with the first fruits of your meditation. And feed the poor in spirit with these fruits. And then shall your barns be filled full in abundance.' That is to say, your inner spiritual nature shall be fulfilled to running over."

What could be more helpful than this advice? To help all mankind by an unconditional love poured out on man just because he exists – this is to free oneself from all the discriminatory judgements which blur the vision and feed the ego. Jesus talked to fools and sinners in the same way that he talked to his disciples, and the Buddha refused to accept the caste system of India and took into his sangha robbers and murderers as well as the good. He treated the rich as being in the same need as the poor, and all because he was, like Jesus, free from the conditioning which ties us to qualifying that word *is*.

To surrender to things as they are, in their isness, is to love them as they are; to love them as they are is to be at one with them. 'See all beings as Buddha, and all places as Nirvana' advises Tibetan scripture. By becoming awakened to the *isness* of creation, we find ourselves in Nirvana – or Heaven – fulfilled to running over, and wonderfully in accord with all beings – human, animal or mere substance. By seeing the totality, we ourselves become total; by finding the wholeness of existence, we ourselves become whole.

Such ways of worship as these are active as well as passive, needing to be given out as well as taken in.

"And if you keep this lovely law and this life-giving advice, if you keep it, then, as Solomon says: 'it shall be life to your soul and the softness of the love of God within and grace to your cheeks without', and your body will bear the radiance in outward form of your inner being. And from these two things, the life within and the radiant action without – for with unerring truth you will respond to all the needs about you – by the teaching of Christ, from these two things hangs all the law and the prophets. For when you are made thus perfect in your integration, both within and without, then you will work confidently because you are grounded in grace, the guide to others, lovingly lifting up your naked blind being to the blissful being of God, one in grace with him, although distinct in nature."

To respond to the needs of others unerringly – this, surely, is the ultimate goal of the spiritual life. First we must find the God-ground and then we must act on it in the world. This is the essential purpose and journey of mankind. If we fail to make ourselves one with the God-ground, feeling it to be the source of all we do, then our actions, however humanitarian, will lack grace for they will stem from ideas and mixed motives and will not always accord with the real situation. And on the other hand, if we do discover the ultimate essence of ourselves and then keep it *to* ourselves thus shutting ourselves away from mankind, we will be guilty of ingratitude and irresponsibility to the created world. In fact shutting up the radiance of the God-ground within oneself is just about impossible. As we grow clearer and clearer of the self-centred motives which dominate our lives, so our loving response to the world is felt more and more deeply as essential action.

Zen Buddhism, with the Bodhisattva path as its basis, has always emphasised selfless action as its goal. Its moment of enlightenment (called *satori*) – which is the equivalent of grace in Christianity, for it is the extraordinary and almost indescribable experience of the dropping of all barriers between subject and object – is also regarded as the start of real life in the world. Until this experience, a person is dominated by duality, the separation between self and other. But after it, although the luminosity of the experience itself may fade, actions proceed more spontaneously from a new consciousness within.

The author of the *Cloud*, with his medieval love of natural similes, perhaps would have enjoyed this account of the process from Zen: At the beginning rivers are rivers and mountains are mountains (when, in our ordinary way, we see all things as separate entities, governing each other and bringing themselves about); then, when we are awakened a little bit, rivers are no longer rivers and mountains are no longer mountains (we then see the essential oneness of their naked essence and being); but when we are fully enlightened we come back to the market place and then rivers are again rivers and mountains are again mountains (because, having come to know their absolute nature, we can now respond in full harmony to their relative, natural qualities).

The other link Zen and Eastern religions have with *The Book of Privy Counselling* is that all of them believe it necessary to follow certain methods (such as mantra) in order to gain a foothold, as it were. The start of practice is the beginning of your journey, the beginning of your awakening.

What brings us, though, to this opening up of the spirit? What is the agency that arouses in us even a vestige of belief that there is some new aspect of existence to be discovered? All religions have the same answer. It is said to be the mysterious and unfathomable working of the God-ground itself: "God must first awaken us", says Swami Ramdas. "It is grace alone in the beginning, in the middle and at the end of our spiritual endeavours. Man in his arrogance says he is able to do all things . . . but he will come to know by experience that by his effort he is not able to do anything. . . . A devotee rightly says, 'O God, I remember you because you remembered me first.' He must draw us towards Him. Then alone we can go to Him. It is just like a needle attracted by a magnet. We must become needles for the divine magnet to draw us towards It. How to become needles? This is possible only by wishing to have Him, aspiring to have Him and Him alone and nothing else in the world." And the Sufi, Bistami, said: 'I fancied that I loved Him . . . but on reflection I saw that His love preceded mine.'

"What you are looking for is what is looking" said St Francis of Assisi.

It seems, then, that we travel in a circle. We are born with an innocent purity of heart, like that of the finer animals. Then as we gain in knowledge and understanding we move away from ourselves and out into the world, where many of us become lost for a long time. But then we are drawn back again to our innermost being, reuniting ourselves with innocence and purity, but now no longer as a child but as a full human being. In order to make this return, though, we must open ourselves up to our own true existence.

"In all of us there dwells a secret marvellous power of freeing ourselves from the changes of time, of withdrawing to our secret selves away from external things, and so discovering to ourselves the eternal in us in the form of unchangeability. This presentation of ourselves to ourselves is the most truly personal experience, upon which depends everything that we know of the suprasensual world. This presentation shows us for the first time what real existence is, whilst all else only appears to be." (Friedrich von Schelling.)

"Although I bid you plainly and boldly to set out in this contemplative work," says *The Book of Privy Counselling*, "nevertheless I feel certain, without error or doubt, that the grace of God is always the chief stirrer and worker, either with your techniques or without. And you or any like you must make yourselves open and receptive to consenting and suffering to such work until you are pure in spirit and discover by the proof of your own spiritual seeing that you are one with God."

In the *Cloud*, he adds: "And so work eagerly awhile and beat upon this high cloud of unknowing and rest later. For unless he is given special grace, he who wants to progress in this work must find it full of great difficulty.

"But, I wonder, why should we consider that work so hard? Surely the stirring of love in our hearts which is by the hand of God is not painful? For God is always ready to work on every person who is disposed towards it and who has prepared himself as best he can for that grace.

"Then wherein is the trouble, I ask you? The difficulty and hard work lies most surely, in treading down the thoughts of all the things in the outside world and in holding them under the cloud of *forgetting*. In this is all the labour; for this is man's struggle which he makes to receive God's grace. But the grace of God – that awakening of the heart to selfless love – that is the work of God alone. And so you prepare yourself in your work and surely I promise you he shall not fail in his."

What work, though, does the author mean? What can we do? As well as mantra, the *Cloud* suggests two techniques for overcoming distractions:

"Do whatever you can to behave as though you did not know that they [thoughts] pressed so hard upon you and between you and God. Try to look, as it were, beyond them and over their shoulders, as though searching for something else, as indeed you are, for that thing is God hidden within a cloud of unknowing. And if you do this, I am certain that within a short time you will be eased of your trouble. I know that if this device is well and truly carried out it is the right one, for it is nothing else but a longing for God, to see and feel him as if he is yourself. And such a desire is real love which always merits peace.

"Another device there is: test it if you want to. When you feel that you can in nowise put your thoughts down, cower beneath them as a captive and a coward overcome in battle, and understand that it is wrong to wear yourself out any longer with them. So give yourself up to God in the midst of your enemies and feel you must give up yourself completely. Take good heed of this advice, I beg you, for the proof of it is that you will then melt in God's hands as though poured out like water. And surely, if you do this properly you will arrive at a true self-knowledge and feeling of yourself as you really are, a wretched and defiled thing far worse than no thing at all. This is the deep experience of humbleness. And when God sees you in your utter humility he will destroy your uneasy thoughts and take you up in his arms as a father does his child who is about to perish under the mouths of wild swine or mad bears, and will cherishingly dry your spiritual tears."

Such a technique, so beautifully described, speaks for itself. When one begins to do it, however, it is perhaps worth remembering that an effective help to looking beyond thoughts is an actual image of the God-ground, on to which you can fasten your eyes. For Buddhists there are many rupas (statues) of the Buddha in different meditational poses and for Christians there are icons or images of Christ. By placing your whole attention on the rupa or image – not taking note of it intellectually, but in a very simple fashion allowing your whole mind to rest upon it – thoughts fall away, and the image itself seems to lose its finiteness and become infinite.

The author's second device deserves a chapter to itself, for to many people the unusual action of abandoning oneself, in deep distress at one's own powerlessness, is indeed a turning point; a moment when a wonderful new sense of being will enter the heart. "Had the saints of the first days any other secret than that of becoming moment by moment what the divine action wished to make of them? And will that divine action not continue to shed its glory until the end of the world on those souls who abandon themselves to it without reserve?" asks Jean de Caussade. "Let Thy word, God, become my life's expression", said Inayat Khan. The sense that one can do nothing on one's own, that everything one does is bewilderingly insufficient, has to be so genuine as to be real suffering. "It is the last painful break with the life of illusion, the tearing away of the self from that world of becoming, in which all its natural affections and desires are rooted, to which its intellect and senses correspond; and the thrusting of it into that world of being where at first, weak and blinded, it can but find a wilderness, a 'dark'", says Evelyn Underhill.

The suffering of powerlessness, which *The Book of Privy Counselling* tells us of, is not only caused by the inability to experience the God-ground but also by the feeling that one is doomed never to do so because of the very fact of one's own bodily existence. "Whenever you look at yourself," the author says, "and see and feel that it is yourself you are experiencing and not God, then be filled with sorrow and heartily long after the feeling of God; evermore desiring, without ceasing, to lose the woeful knowledge and tainted feeling of your blind being; and long to flee from yourself as from venom. Then forsake yourself and disregard yourself as ruthlessly as your Lord bids you. And sometimes when you yearn so intensely – not to un-be, for that would be madness and wrongness in the eyes of God; but to let go the experience and the feeling of yourself, which you must do if God's love shall be perfectly felt by you –

then you seem to see and feel that nothing brings you to that state because there always follows you and accompanies you in your contemplation a naked feeling of your blind being between yourself and God, however hard you try – except occasionally when God will let you experience himself in abundance of love. But except for such an occasion the naked awareness of your blind being will continually press upon you as a barrier between you and God, in the same way as at the beginning of this work the characteristics of your personality were a barrier between you and the direct consciousness of yourself – it is then that you will feel yourself to be a full and heavy burden. . . .

"But in this sorrow, you need to have full caution in this way: you shall be wary in the time of this sorrow that you neither too ruthlessly strain your body nor your spirit, but sit fully still, as it were in a sleeping manner, all deep and shrunken in sorrow. This is true sorrow; this is perfect sorrow; and well were him that might win to this sorrow. All men have matter of sorrow: but most specially he feels matter of sorrow, that believes and feels that he is. All other sorrows be to this in comparison but as it were game to earnest.

"For all the woe there is in the world is nothing to that, because then you are a cross unto yourself. Yet this is the true way to our Lord, as he himself said: 'Let him take up his cross' – the painful burden of himself – that afterwards he will 'follow me' into bliss and on into the mount of perfection – 'tasting the sweetness of my love in the wonderful experience of myself'. Here you may see you must painfully come to be aware of the burden of yourself as a cross before you can be oned with God in the transcendent experience of his being, that which is perfect compassionate love.

"And I ask you now, do you think you will reach this contemplation by the use of your wits? Surely never. Nor yet by your attractive, wise, subtle and clever imagination. . . . I would most surely rather have a blind naked feeling of myself than anything else. Not of my *doings* but of *myself*. Many men call their activities themselves, and it is not so; for I, the doer, am one thing and the deeds that I do are another. And the same it is of God – he is one within himself and his deeds are distinct from him."

Here the author of the *Cloud* has come to one of man's greatest causes of confusion – his false identification with what he does. We identify with our wants and with our loves and hates, with class, status, fame and wealth. A Zen master once called these the "clothes that we wear in between naked birth and naked death, when almost all people are taken in by only these clothes. They think that the entire problem of living is out of all these clothes, which nice ones will they wear? And they never once ask the questions: What is the reality of life?; What is the naked self? In other words . . . the relationship which is determined from the outside and balanced against other people and things is the same as the 'clothes'. . . . We seem to be only concerned with the clothes during the interval when we are alive, or the self which is determined from the outside and it seems that we assume this is all there is in life."

To become conscious of our naked beingness, as was pointed out at the beginning of this chapter, is the arising of consciousness of God; and sorrow at the fact that we *are* is the consciousness which brings us closest to God. In accordance with his teaching on God as the Doer, the author of the *Cloud* continues:

"We may proudly [arrogantly] strain to achieve union only to stumble at the end. For truly without him there is nothing we can do, he himself saying: 'Without me you can do nothing.' You should understand by this that without his first stirring you and being the principal mover of you, and you only the responder with your consent and suffering, you can do nothing in the world that perfectly pleases him.

"I say all this because of the confusion in erring and presumptuous men that because of the cleverness of their learning or their speculative intelligence they themselves are always the principal workers, God but suffering or passively consenting; when in fact the contrary is the truth in all contemplative things."

It is a fact that when we feel god-less and have not consciously experienced the actual feeling of the God-ground, we naturally regard ourselves as the principal doers in the choice of techniques we make, the amount of time we spend on them, and so on. Yet who in the first place suggested we should do all this at all? The answer lies in our own gradual awakening. We are responding to the insistent dimension of the God-ground within us and once the awakening has begun it is very difficult to shut one's eyes again.

Yet for a long time the feeling goes on that *we* are the doers and the choice is ours. In the West particularly we always imagine that we must choose, say, between one religious practice or another and that one will be right and the other wrong. But here the author bids us be more passive – not inactive – but more intuitive with regard to our progress – 'not snatching as if you were a greedy greyhound' – but allowing the practice to suggest itself, expectantly waiting, alert for guidance but not demanding it. In fact this very work of actively waiting produces a depth of understanding in us and a harmony which is likened in Taoism to the flowing course of water – 'nothing in the world is weaker than water, but it has no better in overcoming the hard'.

Soto Zen has an exercise called *shikantaza* in which the mind must become as firmly seated as the body, peacefully unhurried and yet wholly resolute on finding the Buddha-nature (or God-ground) and without a trace of quietism; alert and stretched like a bowstring in an effortless concentrated awareness. This easy and yet intense watchful awareness is likened to the vigilance of a swordsman in a duel. Such an attitude of mind is unmoved by the world about it; it is itself the unmoving centre of all movement. "Abandoning thinking and doing", said Zen master Dogen, echoing the author of the *Cloud*, "is nothing other than every form of doing and acting."

Surrendering to the working of a higher power within us helps us to drop the isolated sense of separate selfhood which itself is the greatest barrier to unity with the God-ground, for surrender means a continuous giving up of self-centred identity. Indeed the sensation that there is no self to perform one's acts may be a great moment of insight, a miraculous release, a feeling of having dropped a heavy and unnecessary burden – the sea rises and falls and the wind blows but not because of me; in the same way the legs are moved, the food is eaten, the book is read, but no self is involved.

Thomas Merton, in his preface to the *Bhagavadgita*, said: "Realisation of the Supreme Player whose Play is manifested in the million-formed, inexhaustible richness of beings and events, is what gives us the key to the meaning of life. Once we live in awareness of the cosmic dance and move in time with the Dancer, our life attains its true dimension. It is at once more serious and less serious than the life of one who does not sense this inner cosmic dynamism. To live without this illuminated consciousness is to live as a beast of burden, carrying one's life with tragic seriousness as a huge, incomprehensible weight. The weight of the burden is the seriousness with which one takes one's own individual and separate self. To live with the true consciousness of life centred in Another is to lose one's self-important seriousness and thus to live life as 'play' in union with a Cosmic Player. It is He alone that one takes seriously. But to take Him seriously is to find joy and spontaneity in everything, for everything is gift and grace. In other words, to live selfishly is to bear life as an intolerable burden. To live selflessly is to live in joy, realising by experience that life itself is love and gift. To be a lover and a giver is to be a channel through which the Supreme Giver manifests His love in the world.''

The author of the *Cloud* wanted it to be clear, however, that in contemplation there should be complete surrender, but in daily life there should be initiative from man. He defined it in this way: "Nevertheless in an ordered and active life man's knowledge and his natural common sense shall work together with God in proper order; God's consent and assistance being experienced through earthly witnesses – the wisdom of scripture, reliable advice, and the understanding of natural common sense which takes into account one's condition such as age and circumstances of life. In fact, man should not follow the impulse of his mind, however desirable and even holy it might seem, until he knows it to be strongly supported by all or any one of those three witnesses. . . .

"And since all men in this life can be divided into three groups – sinners [people still ignorant of God], actives, and contemplatives – the word of our Lord can be said to all: 'Without me you can do nothing.' In sinners he is suffering passively with them for they must do as they will; in actives he is both passively present and actively assisting them; in contemplatives he is more than all this, for he is the principal actor himself, awakening and moving them to his divine being."

How are we to know that we are following the true path? Many people are troubled by this doubt, for so often our natural confidence in ourselves has been sapped by an overdose of intellectualism and an underdose of intuition. The author of the *Cloud* gives a clear description of what we shall find in ourselves to confirm our way. First he tells us that there are two signs we can be sure of: one is a growing desire for contemplation (known as meditation in Eastern religion) which begins to dominate our everyday activities and which brings about increasing insight; and the other is a stirring in our mind of happiness whenever we read about things of the spirit. These two together are certain signs that we are on the right path.

"And if your eager liking for reading and hearing of this matter is so abounding in itself that it goes with you to bed and accompanies you all day, pulling you away from your usual concerns and coming between you and the world, linking itself so much with your heart that you are no longer aware of it as a separate desire . . . then your inward evidence and also your outer are both in accord and knitting together in one. For then your whole manner will be transformed and your face will radiate joy and become beautiful. While it lasts all things are pleasing to you and life seems easy with all griefs no longer working in you. A thousand miles would you run to talk to someone who you knew really felt it; and yet when you got there you could find no words adequate. And whatever conversation others hold you will only want to speak of *it*. Few will be your words but full of fruitfulness and fire: a short sentence from you will contain a world of wisdom yet may seem mere nonsense to others who are still bound up in their own minds. Your silence will be tranquil, your speech helpful and your realisation deep within your being. Your self-confidence will be spontaneously pure, your manner of speaking gentle, your sense of humour merry, and your delight in everything will be like the play of a child. You will love solitude and be off by yourself, knowing that others would hinder you unless they too shared your attraction to God. You will no longer want to read books or hear about such work because you only want the direct experience of it – the inward evidence of the outer – which is the proof that you are in accord with the way of God."

And at the end of *The Book of Privy Counselling*, our author tells us:

"And to this great experience shall you come by that way which I have told you of, and by relying on God's grace to help you and to lead you. And the way I have told you of is that you should evermore without ceasing strive for the naked awareness of yourself, constantly offering up your being to God as the most precious offering that you can make. But take care, as I have said before, that it is naked, for fear that you will deceive yourself. If this awareness is truly naked then it will be full painful to you in the beginning to remain like that for any time because, as I have explained, your reason and intellect will find no meat for themselves in it. Let them fast awhile, I beg you, from their own natural delight in the things they know. For it is true that a man naturally wants to understand; but at the same time no amount of knowledge or learning will bring him to taste the actual experience of God, for only grace can do this. And so I urge you, seek more after experience than after knowledge. For knowledge will often deceive you, knowledge inflates you, but love builds you truly. Knowing is hard work, but loving is serene rest."

Bibliography

Allen, Warner. *The Timeless Moment* (London, 1946)

Ancelet-Hustache, Jeanne. *Master Eckhart and the Rhineland Mystics* (London, undated)

Arberry, A. J. *Sufism* (London, 1950)

Augustine, St. *Confessions* (numerous editions)

Bancroft, Anne. *Modern Mystics and Sages* (London, 1978)
       Religions of the East (London, 1974)
       Zen: Direct Pointing to Reality (London, 1980)

Berdyaev, N. *Freedom and Spirit* (London, 1935)

Bernard, St. *The Book of St. Bernard on the Love of God* ed. E. G. Gardner (London, undated)
    The Letters of Saint Bernard of Clairvaux ed. B. Scott James (London, 1957)
    The Steps of Humility by Bernard, Abbot of Clairvaux ed. G. B. Burch (Harvard, 1940)

Bhagavad-Gita ed. Swami Prabhavananda and Christopher Isherwood (California, 1944)
    trans. Swami Bhaktivedanta: with preface by Thomas Merton (London, 1963)

Blofeld, John. *The Wheel of Life* (London, 1959)

Butler, Dom Cuthbert. *Western Mysticism* (London, 1960)

Capra, Fritjof. *The Tao of Physics* (London, 1975)

Caussade, Jean-Pierre de. *Self-Abandonment to Divine Providence* (London, 1959)

Cloud of Unknowing, the. The Cloud of Unknowing and the Book of Privy Counselling ed. William Johnston (New York, 1973)
    The Cloud of Unknowing, Epistle of Privy Counsel and Denis Hid Divinity ed. Dom Justin McCann (London, 1924)
    The Cloud of Unknowing ed. Evelyn Underhill (London, 1956)
    The Cloud of Unknowing trans. Clifton Wolters (London, 1961)

Comper, Frances. *Richard Rolle* (London, 1928)

Davies, Penelope. *Country Life in the Middle Ages* (London, 1972)

Dionysius the Areopagite. *On the Divine Names and the Mystical Theology* trans. C. E. Rolt (London, 1920)

Eckhart, Meister. *Meister Eckhart* trans. Raymond B. Blakney (New York, 1941)

Meister Eckhart, Vol. I trans. C. de B. Evans (London, 1956)

Meister Eckhart, Sermons and Treatises, Vol. I trans. M. O'C. Walshe (London, 1979)

Gilson, Etienne. *The Mystical Theology of St. Bernard* (London, 1940)

Graef, Hilda. *The Light and the Rainbow* (London, 1959)

Huxley, Aldous. *The Perennial Philosophy* (London, 1946)

Inge, W. R. *Christian Mysticism* (London, 1899)

Jones, Rufus. *Studies in Mystical Religion* (London, 1909)

Julian of Norwich. *A Book of Showings to the Anchoress Julian of Norwich, Parts One and Two* ed. Edmund Colledge and James Walsh (Toronto, 1980)

The Revelations of Divine Love of Julian of Norwich ed. James Walsh (London, 1961)

A Shewing of God's Love ed. Anna Maria Reynolds (London, 1958)

Kapleau, Philip. *Three Pillars of Zen* (Boston, 1965)

Khan, Inayat. *The Way of Illumination* (London, undated)

Kingsland, William. *An Anthology of Mysticism and Mystical Philosophy* (London, 1927)

Lao Tzu. *Tao Te Ching* (many editions)

McKisack, May. *The Fourteenth Century* (Oxford, 1959)

Merton, Thomas. *The Last of the Fathers* (New York, 1954)

Mystics and Zen Masters (New York, 1961)

Seeds of Contemplation (London, 1972)

Zen and the Birds of Appetite (New York, 1968)

Molinari, Paul. *Julian of Norwich* (London, undated)

Otto, Rudolf. *Mysticism East and West* (London, 1932)

Patanjali. *How to know God; the Yoga Aphorisms of Patanjali* trans. Swami Prabhavananda and Christopher Isherwood (London, 1953)

Plotinus. *The Essence of Plotinus* trans. G. H. Turnbull (New York, 1934)

Ramana Maharshi. *The Teachings of Ramana Maharshi* ed. Arthur Osborne (London, 1962)

Ramdas, Swami. *In Quest of God* (Bombay, undated)

Rolle, Richard. *The Amending of Life* trans. R. Misyn (London, 1927)

The Fire of Love and the Mending of Life ed. Frances M. M. Comper (London, 1914)

The Form of Perfect Living ed. G. Hodgson (London, 1910)

The Psalter ed. H. R. Bramley (Oxford, 1884)

Selected Works of Richard Rolle ed. G. C. Heseltine (London, 1930)

Rops, Daniel. *Bernard of Clairvaux* (London, 1964)

Ruysbroeck, Jan van. *The Adornment of the Spiritual Marriage, The Book of Truth, The Sparkling Stone* trans. P. Wynschenk Dom (London, 1916)

The Twelve Beguines trans. J. Francis (London, 1913)

Sasaki, Joshu. *Buddha is the Center of Gravity* (New Mexico, 1974)

Schürmann, Reiner. *Meister Eckhart, Mystic and Philosopher* (Indiana, 1978)

Bibliography

Scott James, B. *Saint Bernard of Clairvaux* (London, 1957)

Steiner, Rudolf. *Eleven European Mystics* (New York, 1971)

Suzuki, D. T. *Mysticism Christian and Buddhist* (London, 1957)

Thouless, Robert H. *The Lady Julian* (London, undated)

Underhill, Evelyn. *Mysticism* (London, 1960)
> *Mystics of the Church* (London, undated)
> *Ruysbroeck* (London, 1915)

Watts, Alan. *Beyond Theology* (London, 1964)
> *The Supreme Identity* (New York, 1972)
> *The Way of Zen* (London, 1957)

Way of a Pilgrim trans. R. M. French (London, 1965)

Williams, Harry. *True Resurrection* (London, 1972)

Williams, W. W. *The Mysticism of St. Bernard* (London, 1931)
> *Studies in Bernard of Clairvaux* (London, 1927)

Zukav, Gary. *The Dancing Wu Li Masters* (London, 1979)

Index